Towards Organizational Fitness

Dedicated to Edna and Tangy

Towards Organizational Fitness

A Guide to Diagnosis and Treatment

GERRY RANDELL
and
JOHN TOPLIS

GOWER

Published by
Gower Publishing Limited
Wey Court East
Union Road
Farnham
Surrey, GU9 7PT
England

Gower Publishing Company
110 Cherry Street
Suite 3-1
Burlington, VT 05401-3818
USA

www.gowerpublishing.com

British Library Cataloguing in Publication Data
A catalogue record for this book is available from the British Library

ISBN: 978 1 4724 2262 0 (hbk)
ISBN: 978 1 4724 2263 7 (ebk – ePDF)
ISBN: 978 1 4724 2264 4 (ebk – ePUB)

Library of Congress Cataloging-in-Publication Data
Randell, G.A. (Gerald Anthony)
  Towards organizational fitness : a guide to diagnosis and treatment / by Gerry Randell and John Toplis.
    pages cm
  Includes bibliographical references and index.
  ISBN 978-1-4724-2262-0 (hbk) -- ISBN 978-1-4724-2263-7 (ebk) -- ISBN 978-1-4724-2264-4 (epub) 1. Organizational change. 2. Problem solving. 3. Corporate culture. 4. Organization--Evaluation. I. Toplils, John. II. Title.
  HD58.8.R348 2014
  658.4'06--dc23

                                                                    2013048302

MIX
Paper from
responsible sources
FSC   FSC® C013985
www.fsc.org

Printed in the United Kingdom by Henry Ling Limited, at the Dorset Press, Dorchester, DT1 1HD

Contents

List of Figures   *vii*
About the Authors   *ix*
Preface   *xi*
Acknowledgments   *xiii*

1   The Need for Organizational Diagnosis and Treatment   1

2   The Lure of 'Fashionable Solutions'   13

3   Describing and Understanding How Organizations Work   23

4   Preparing to Diagnose and Manage Problems   35

5   Diagnosis   51

6   Identifying and Evaluating Possible Strategies and Treatments   67

7   Towards Organizational Fitness   77

8   Leadership – The First Key to Organizational Fitness   97

9   Internal Communications – The Second Key to Organizational
     Fitness   111

10   The Way Ahead   123

Appendix A   Signs and Signals of Organizational Illness and Health   133
Appendix B   When Individuals Threaten the Future of the Organization   141

Notes on Chapters   145

Index   *155*

The Origin of Our Approach

We have now to consider according to what method these complex effects, compounded of the effects of many causes, are to be studied; how we are enabled to trace each effect to the concurrence of causes in which it originated, and ascertain the conditions of its recurrence, the circumstances in which it may be expected again to occur.

John Stuart Mill (1851). *A System of Logic, Ratiocinative and Inductive. Vol. I, Third edition*, page 456. London: John Parker.

List of Figures

3.1	The world of work and management	26
3.2	An open system for analysing behaviour at work	28
5.1	A closed system of the main interactions and problems between individuals, managers and society	60
5.2	A framework for organizational diagnosis	62
5.3	A diagnostic model for people management	63
10.1	Interpreting the results of multivariate analysis	128
10.2	A multivariate analysis system for organizational diagnosis – MASOD	129

About the Authors

G.A. Randell, B.Sc., M.Sc., Ph.D., C.Pychol., F.B.Ps.S.

Gerry Randell is an Emeritus Professor of the University of Bradford. Previously he was Professor of Organisational Behaviour at the Bradford School of Management; Lecturer in Occupational Psychology at Birkbeck College, University of London; Research Psychologist for J. Lyons; and the Industrial Psychologist for LEO Computers.

He is the recipient of the British Psychological Society's Professional Practice Board's Lifetime Achievement Award, as well as the Division of Occupational Psychology LTAA. He has been Chairman of the Occupational Psychology Section of the British Psychological Society; the British representative on the Executive Committee of the International Association of Applied Psychology; the Editor of *The International Review of Applied Psychology*; Assessor to the Civil Service Selection Board; Organizer/President of the 20th Congress of Applied Psychology held in Edinburgh in 1982; Chairman of the Council of the Independent Assessment and Research Centre, London; Advisor to the Governments of Algeria and Singapore; and the Universities of Singapore, Mauritius, Royal Roads BC Canada, and Utara, Malaysia.

He has been consultant to many public and commercial organizations throughout the world. His book, *Staff Appraisal: A First Step to Effective Leadership*, went through four editions and has been translated into Spanish.

J.W. Toplis, B.Sc., C. Psychol., A.B.Ps.S., Chartered M.I.P.D

John Toplis is also a recipient of the Division of Occupational Psychology Lifetime Achievement Award, and is a former Chairman of the Society's Occupational Psychology Section. Since retirement from full-time work he has specialized in the assessment of candidates for top posts in charities and other not-for-profit organizations. He held a number of senior posts at the Post Office and Royal Mail including Head of Psychological Services in the Post Office,

Head of Consultancy Services and subsequently Management Development Advisor in the Training and Development Group, and Head of Training and Development in Royal Mail Anglia. Prior to that he was Director of the Occupational Psychology Unit at Barking College of Technology.

After graduating from Hull University he joined the staff of the National Institute of Industrial Psychology where he led projects on the selection of computer staff before becoming Head of Diagnostic Studies. While at the NIIP he studied at Birkbeck College where Gerry Randell was one of his lecturers.

John has experienced the private, public and not-for-profit sectors as an employee, a consultant and a volunteer. He has worked with leading commercial organizations and consultants, as well as being a magistrate, a school governor and the secretary of a group which succeeded in overturning a controversial planning decision at a Judicial Review Appeal. In May 2013 he became the Chair of the Essex and Ipswich Branch of the Chartered Institute of Personnel and Development.

Preface

This book is aimed at thinking, experienced managers who are concerned about the fitness of their work organization. While it is primarily aimed at those working in organizations offering paid employment, much of the content is relevant to those working in voluntary organizations, clubs and societies.

It is not an academic text book, nor a high-powered exposition of management theory. It is an attempt to bring together ideas about how organizations work and what can be done to help them work better. It hopes to help practising managers with their 'thinking through' and understanding of what is really going on in their organization and to direct them towards what can be done to make the organization fitter for purpose, healthier and a better place for people to work in.

Organizational diagnosis and treatments have a very long history. While this book touchs on the history and accumulated literature it does not attempt any detailed analysis nor assessment of them. Instead, it distils this knowledge in the light of the authors' academic, practitioner and consultancy experiences into what we think is the essence of the issues in order to help thoughtful, concerned managers grapple with the difficulties involved in organizational diagnosis, treatment and development, which are such crucial and demanding components of their work and responsibility.

Gerry Randell and John Toplis

Acknowledgments

This book has been a long time in the making, consequently very many colleagues, students, clients and friends have played a part in the process, too many to list. However, a special acknowledgment must be made of the staff and students of the Human Resources Research Group at the University of Bradford Management Centre from 1970–97, in particular Roger Gill, Colin Ingleton, Alistair Ostell, Dave Taylor and Peter Wright. Their intellectual stimulation and friendship was influential and is greatly valued.

More recently Joe Hawkins has put much expertise into transforming primitive diagrams into elegant figures. The editorial staff of Gower have given considerable help in getting this book knocked into a presentable and grammatical shape.

Gerry Randell

I first proposed a systematic approach to Organizational Diagnosis and Treatment in the Jubilee Volume of Occupational Psychology in 1970. Since then that view has been confirmed in my work as an adviser, consultant, manager and volunteer. I was therefore delighted to learn that Gerry Randell had been working on this book and to have the opportunity to contribute to it.

Many people have influenced my contributions, again too many to list. But my time in the Post Office and Royal Mail gave me many insights and I would particularly like to thank Peter Butcher, Jim Anderson, Richard Osmond, Helena Rozga and David Prince for their support and friendship. I have also learned from Simon Barrow, Iris Cerny, David Lale and Ros Searle as well as from valued clients such as Iain Henderson and Marilyn DeBattista.

Finally, my thanks to Drs Robert Colby and Ruth Marshall who gave me interesting and useful insights into their work as general practitioners in the National Health Service.

John Toplis

Chapter 1
The Need for Organizational Diagnosis and Treatment

Organizations dominate our lives. From the family, through work, play, religions and government their impact on our everyday life and well-being is total. This book is about how organizations can identify and treat processes that constrain them from working at their best and so move them towards being healthy, productive and great places to be a part of.

Work organizations can lose their fitness and become sick, just as people can. This is not surprising as organizations are made of people. Like people, organizations can become both physically and behaviourally sick. Physically sick when plant and equipment breaks down or the money runs out, or the markets disappear, behaviourally sick when the resources are badly managed or the staff becomes alienated, or both.

What is perhaps more surprising is just how much the behavioural sicknesses of organizations reflect the behavioural illnesses of people. People get old and tired, slow down and become far less effective than when they were young, thrusting and energetic. So, too, do organizations. People seek ways to retain their youth and energy, to somehow compensate for the natural effects of ageing. So, too, do organizations. People become ill through the effects of experiences, just every day or traumatic, or due to the onset of internal physiological changes. Organizations can become unhealthy because of an accumulation of 'baggage' from their experiences, for example, their internal systems, through external pressures, competition, legislation and economic conditions as well as chance traumatic events. Organizations can starve when they are deprived of sufficient people, cash, investment, plant, equipment and markets. As with all starvation this can be a long, slow, debilitating process and leads to sickness and even death; for a commercial organization this is bankruptcy.

In contrast, organizations display fitness when they are seen to be healthy, productive, adaptive, flexible and happy places to work in. There is a 'buzz' about them, people want to work there and customers seek their products or services. They are discussed, admired and even honoured.

This book addresses two main issues: First, how to investigate and manage problems involving people at work – a task analogous to that of a medical doctor working with a sick patient. Just as those involved in sport at a high level need to be free of illness or injury to give of their best, so organizations need to diagnose and treat their problems before they aim at a high level of fitness. Second, this book addresses processes associated with organizational fitness – a task analogous to that of a medical doctor who advises a patient on steps that they might take to achieve fitness.

The investigation of problems to ascertain causes is known as *Diagnosis*. Problems involving people at work, such as difficulties in attracting and retaining staff, can have a number of possible causes and making the wrong decision about the causes and applying inappropriate solutions may not only cost money but actually make things worse.

Indeed, diagnosis is at the core of the work of medical doctors, but if we explore what doctors actually do there are some important differences between their work and the work of those involved in organizational diagnosis. At best medical doctors can take stock of a pattern of symptoms in a patient and recognize the illness, disease or other condition using their own experience or the descriptions made by other doctors. A medical doctor can often go on to select a treatment whose efficacy has been recorded by others in their profession. That said, conversations with medical doctors suggest that much of their time may be spent treating and managing symptoms and making sure that they are not signs of something much more serious, without coming to a firm view about diagnosis.

At present there is no agreed taxonomy for recording problems which involve people at work, let alone agreed procedures for recording the efficacy of treatments. We give our views about how matters might be improved in the final chapter of this book. But in the meantime there is the issue of what can be done now and this is what this book is about.

The ultimate aim of this book is to offer guidelines on how to assess and develop the capability and fitness of organizations. Just as a person who is free from illness may not be fit, so an organization that is free from major problems may have little resilience when faced with commercial and other pressures.

Finally, because this is a practical guide written for practising managers and others wishing to develop relevant skills, rather than a conventional text book for students and academics, references to academic and other literature have not been made in the text.

Instead we have put a separate section, 'Notes on Chapters', following the Appendices. This will let readers know 'where we are coming from', research and publications that underpin our messages and where a reader should go to carry forward the ideas and proposals in this book.

An Overview of Our Approach

Information in books is usually presented sequentially. This can be helpful if the material is also sequential as in a story, but is less helpful when there is a need to see the contents as a whole, to consider the contents of several chapters together or to cross reference between chapters. Accordingly, there follows a brief summary of our approach and the contents of the chapters so that readers can obtain an overview of our proposals and identify the chapters of most relevance to the issues that they are considering.

THE LURE OF 'FASHIONABLE SOLUTIONS' (CHAPTER 2)

The history of organizational management contains all manner of 'treatments' for organizational ills and for improving organizational health. They include Robert Owen's 'silent monitors' in 1810, Titus Salt's 'care in the community' in the 1880s, Frederick Winslow Taylor's 'scientific management' and Frank Bunker Gilbreth's 'motion study' at the turn of that century are all examples of nineteenth century 'cures'. The twentieth century proliferated even more.

None can be said to be 'instant', and while some are relatively quick to implement, others, such as Titus Salt's care in the community and the housing schemes associated with chocolate manufacturers such as Cadbury and a soapmaker such as Lever, involved considerable expense. Accordingly they are better described as 'fashionable'.

More recently there has been a spate of books in which authors analyse the features of apparently successful companies and television programmes in which a management 'guru' studies an ailing company or organization and then puts forward proposals to improve its performance. And there have been the views of politicians that either 'privatization' or 'nationalization' would be the best way of running utility and other major service companies.

Does anyone really think that all organizational ills can be cured at a stroke or by a single approach? In any case, few organizations would want all of their employees to be creative, energetic and smiling all the time – even characteristics generally viewed as being positive can have downsides if present in excess. Hopefully some thinking managers and their advisors will have started to question such simplistic thinking. This book aims to help them to do better.

This chapter gives further details of fashionable solutions and then offers a detailed taxonomy of 'treatments' based on whether they are directed at structure or behaviour, their cost and invasiveness. We conclude by making the case for implementing and evaluating relatively mild and inexpensive treatments in the first instance.

DESCRIBING AND UNDERSTANDING HOW ORGANIZATIONS WORK (CHAPTER 3)

This chapter offers models to help describe organizations and explain how they work. The models are derived from systems theory, they are both 'open' and 'closed'.

For anything to be managed, changed, mended or treated, an understanding of how it works is required. Can medical doctors cure an illness without understanding how bodies work? However, the fringes of the world of work are populated by managers, consultants, academics and even 'gurus' who, for a fee, will study and write a report on an organization. Their understanding of how organizations work more often than not is just based on their personal experiences. There are also many 'amateurs' around, cowboy repair men, witch doctors and the like, who sometimes get lucky when kicking a car, thumping the case of a computer or even dosing a patient and getting them back to working order without any real understanding of how or why. What if medical consultants went about their business that way?

Organizations are clearly diverse in terms of their size, ownership, functions and many other characteristics. But just as all the diverse species in the animal kingdom can be described by focusing on the systems that they have in common (such as the cardiovascular and gastroenterological systems) so too are many systems common to all work organizations.

Also, organizations are rarely independent entities, they exist within a culture. If the organization's environment is itself sick, if the culture or society in which it is trying to exist and prosper is malevolent, it will be much harder to achieve organizational fitness. In such circumstances, what (if anything) can be done becomes a big political, sociological or even a theological issue, outside the scope of this book. However, beware the mindset that attributes too quickly and blames all an organization's ills on external factors. People have found ways of working together to make things better under the most dreadful circumstances.

So in this chapter we propose a 'systems' approach for describing, analysing and understanding behaviour at work that brings together all the variables within and impinging upon work organizations. In particular two models are put forward and discussed in detail: 'The world of work and management' (a 'closed' system) and 'An open system for analysing behaviour at work' (an 'open' system).

Both 'closed' and 'open' systems are proposed because account needs to be taken of the way that work organizations are dependent on the society and culture within which they exist. We hope that the proposed systems will aid those seeking to diagnose problems and improve fitness and will lay a foundation for others to build on.

PREPARING TO DIAGNOSE AND MANAGE PROBLEMS (CHAPTER 4)

The next three chapters are about examining, diagnosing, managing problems which are adverseley affecting organizational health and how to plan and staff these activities. While this chapter focuses on the initial stages of preparing to diagnose and manage problems we advise that all three chapters should be read before any diagnostic work is planned. Just as there are many signs and symptoms of an individual's illness, there are also many indicators of unhealthy organizations. They include measures of behaviour at work, of performance at work, of the attributes of employees and how people feel about their work, we give examples of each. Further indicators of how people feel about their work are listed in Appendix A, they can be assessed by observation and by seeking the views of employees.

We suggest that there are currently two main approaches to the systematic diagnosis of problems. The first is to identify any departures from good practice, while the second is to look back over time to see if there were times when things were better – or even worse – and look for associated changes which may explain the variations. Approaches that may be developed in the future are described in Chapter 10.

Drawing on the approach of medical doctors to diagnosis, we suggest a series of questions to yield information about the diagnosis, management and perhaps treatment of problems and the subsequent monitoring. We suggest that an iterative cycle of activities may need to be repeated until the problem is resolved and suggest and discuss eight questions to be considered when the first stage, the collection of information, is taking place.

Because managers and others will want to know how long an investigation will take and how it can be staffed and funded, we discuss these issues. In particular, we suggest that a preliminary investigation might be helpful.

Finally, the expertise required by staff involved in all stages of organizational diagnosis and management is discussed together with comments about the potential sources of such staff both within and outside an organization. In particular, we view the potential involvement of an organization's top management as a 'mixed blessing'. On the one hand they may have additional relevant background information, and may also be able to see how possible remedial action may complement or conflict with other policies and procedures. On the other hand they may lack diagnostic skills, and the information collected may be raising questions or concerns about areas for which they are responsible. All in all, staffing decisions can require some shrewd judgements.

DIAGNOSIS (CHAPTER 5)

In our view organizational diagnosis should comprise: (a) the preparation for organizational diagnosis (discussed in Chapter 4); (b) diagnosis itself (discussed in detail in this chapter) and (c) the systematic assessment of possible treatments (Chapter 6). It is likely that these three phases will overlap.

This chapter deals mainly with organizational diagnosis itself. We first discuss how much time should be spent on diagnosis. Then, after presenting a short history of organizational diagnosis, we present three scenarios to illustrate how organizational diagnoses were carried out and recommendations made, in these scenarios the recommendations made were based directly on the results of the investigation. In other words both nature and cause were established.

We then discuss what can be learned about diagnosis from considering these scenarios. Our conclusions are:

1.   That local diagnoses may not have been attempted or may not be correct.

2.   That those who collect diagnostic information do not need to have expertise in diagnosis.

3.   Some problems can be traced to specific locations or groups.

4.   That there are ways of thinking that can help to link symptoms with their causes.

5.   That more use might be made of historical information.

We conclude this chapter by presenting and discussing a systems approach to organizational diagnosis. This includes two models, 'A closed system of the main interactions and problems between individuals, managers and society'; and 'A framework for organizational diagnosis'. We suggest that the first decision that a diagnostic team has to make is whether the malaise or other problem being diagnosed is primarily structural, that is, the management structure and responsibilities, or behavioural, the attitudes, inclinations and skills of the managers, or lack of them. The key point is made that the diagnosis may reveal many things that are 'wrong' in the organization and that they cannot be put 'right' by a single treatment. The crucial decision then has to be made, what treatment needs to be applied *next*?

Finally a further model is put forward, 'A diagnostic model for people management', to start the process of diagnosis at the level of individuals making up the organization.

IDENTIFYING AND EVALUATING POSSIBLE STRATEGIES AND TREATMENTS (CHAPTER 6)

There is now the issue of which treatments, or combination of treatments, to apply. Having made clear that 'treatments' do not need to be restricted to a single action, we report three scenarios in some detail to show how this was done in practice.

In the first scenario the treatment was in direct response to the diagnostic information collected. In the second, 'remedial action' was required which went beyond being a simple response to the criticisms made. The third scenario was one in which multiple problems were identified.

The second part of this chapter considers how to consider and take action, and finally discusses evaluation – not just of the treatment but of the whole series of processes described in Chapters 4–6 ranging from the initial problem investigation to diagnosis and eventual treatment.

TOWARDS ORGANIZATIONAL FITNESS (CHAPTER 7)

In our view, an organization is fit if it is ready at all times to handle issues or take up opportunities as they arise. We suggest that there are at least five possible ways of moving forward. The first is to encourage local dialogue about possible ways of improving fitness. The second is to use surveys and audits to obtain additional information. The third is to use organizational change to stimulate fitness. The fourth is to adopt a systematic 'Top-down' approach, using a combination of methods and measures. Finally, there is the possibility of a 'Bottom-up' approach, again using a combination of methods and measures.

In discussing each approach, particular attention is paid to the 'Top-down' approach, partly because it is similar to the problem-solving approach described the Chapters 4–6, and partly because of its common (but often unsuccessful) use in organizations. The Bottom-up approach is also discussed in detail because this approach can have benefits in terms of employee engagement.

Following a discussion of 'Where to Start' we move on to discuss the staffing of an organizational fitness initiative and the long term management of a Fitness Programme.

LEADERSHIP – THE FIRST KEY TO ORGANIZATIONAL FITNESS (CHAPTER 8)

We are still a long way off consensus about the exact nature of leadership. There appears to be a tendency to regard leadership as a 'thing' that some people possess. In our view this approach is misguided.

The leadership literature displays that a considerable amount of research has been done on the *cognitive*, that is, what a leader needs to know or even be! A fair amount has been done on the *perceptual*, that is, what a leader needs to see, hear, sense, have 'vision' with different kinds of followers in different kinds of situations. However, relatively little systematic work has been done on the *motor*, how a leader behaves, sounds and looks. But for some notable exceptions, these so-called 'micro-processes' of leadership have been neglected by researchers and practitioners alike. The reasons for this apparent neglect are discussed.

As a result of research it is suggested that leadership should be defined as a skill and the practical implications of this are discussed. In our view, what needs to be established is a catalogue of essential behaviours for leaders that would be trainable. Those that were critical but not trainable would then be the province of the management selector rather than the leadership developer. The elusive solid core, the essential components, of all leadership appears to be the verbal and non-verbal behaviour required for *collecting information, giving information, influencing behaviour* and *handling emotion*. The chapter stresses that, to become an effective leader, senior and other managers require training in these 'micro-skills'.

Because of the difference that skilled leadership can make and because leaders are also often involved in both the diagnosis and treatment of organizational problems and in raising the standards of organizational fitness, it is our view that skilled leadership is a key element in resolving organizational ills and improving fitness, while unskilled leadership is likely to be a dominant cause of ills.

INTERNAL COMMUNICATIONS – THE SECOND KEY TO ORGANIZATIONAL FITNESS (CHAPTER 9)

In this chapter we draw attention to further matters which may not be given sufficient attention and which may not be apparent if investigations are focused within work groups. It concerns internal communications and the related matter of co-ordination. This is because organizational fitness is not just to do with relationships within groups, but also to do with groups working together. When organization-wide surveys have been carried out, one of the areas most heavily criticized has been 'internal communications'.

Most organizations attempt to make changes through 'Top-down' Deployment, but problems are legion and we give examples and possible reasons. We then go on to suggest how successful deployment can be planned by identifying and discussing eight stages.

Next we discuss how 'Bottom-up' communications might be improved, before discussing communications between work-groups. While information about whether and how work-groups are co-ordinating their activities is sometimes collected by academic and other researchers, its potential for wider use has yet to be fully explored or appreciated.

We end the chapter by making the case for co-ordinating all change in an organization and discuss who might be responsible for doing this. We conclude that each organization must find the best way of doing this that meets its needs.

THE WAY AHEAD (CHAPTER 10)

In this final chapter we identify three ways ahead that would enhance the whole process of organizational diagnosis and treatment. First it is proposed that a 'Manual for Organizational Diagnosis' should be developed that would contain a classification of all organizational ills and the treatments available that would make them fit and healthy. Attention is drawn to how this has been achieved in another scientific field. The manual might contain a list of 'Signs and Signals of Organizational Sickness and Health' along the lines of Appendix A. It might list and categorize all the sicknesses that organizations can suffer from. Further, it might list and categorize all possible treatments and give details of checklists developed by different types and sizes of organization to aid information collection and diagnosis.

The second proposal is for the development of statistical 'evidence-based' diagnosis, which will make use of 'multivariate analysis'. Packages of computer programs are already available and work on simulation and modelling has already started. Illustrative results are given, and what now needs to be done is outlined. It is anticipated that, in time, work organizations will be able to make more statistically based, rather than intuition based, decisions on what the organization should be doing differently *next* to make them more productive and a better place to work in.

The third proposal involves setting up a new profession, Professional Organizational Diagnosticians, who would be experts in assembling and analysing information made available to them by managers and then using multivariate analysis to find out what exactly is going on in the organization and how it can be improved.

The development of an evidence-based approach should further improve the quality of diagnosis. However, until that has been developed the main part of this book has described and discussed approaches to improving organizational fitness that are already available to people who want to make things better in their organization.

Chapter 2
The Lure of 'Fashionable Solutions'

This chapter outlines some of the various ways over history that work organizations have used to treat their organizational ills and improve their organizational health. Some current approaches are then categorized as to whether or not they are structural or behavioural in their effect. Then, we offer a further classification along a scale of invasiveness/cost from the most intrusive and expensive, the 'mega' through 'macro', 'midi', 'mini' to the cheap and cheerful 'micro'.

A History of Fashionable Solutions

Since the dawn of managerial history work organizations have sought ways to improve the performance of staff in their jobs. They have gone about this in many ways, more often than not based on the personal beliefs or philosophy of those in charge or, less commendably, what is currently in favour in other organizations, the 'flavour of the month', fashionable, approach.

The history of organizational management contains all manner of 'treatments' for organizational ills and for improving organizational health, from Matthew Boulton's and James Watt Jr.'s managerial innovations at the turn of the eighteenth century (1799) to Robert Owen's model village in New Lanark, Scotland and his 'silent monitors' in the 1810s, Titus Salt's 'care in the community' in Bradford, Yorkshire, in the 1880s, to Frederick Winslow Taylor's 'scientific management' and Frank Bunker Gilbreth's 'method study' in the USA are all examples of nineteenth-century 'cures'. The twentieth century proliferated even more, Training Within Industry, Management by Objectives, Performance Appraisal, Payment by Results, Quality Circles, Total Quality Management, Investors in People, Business Process Engineering etc., all given their acronyms for easy digestion and promulgation. Many of these have been applied not necessarily to cure a specific ill but in the hope and expectation of improving organizational 'fitness'.

All these treatments may produce benefits for either management or employees, and sometimes both. But the introduction and maintenance of the schemes can involve significant costs and have other 'downsides'. Further, they are directed at different aspects of work, for example, F.W. Taylor's 'scientific management' focused on the way that work should be timed, Frank and Lillian Gilbreth showed the best movements that tasks require, Robert Owen's 'silent monitors' encouraged individual effort, while Titus Salt provided a high standard of accommodation and care, for those days, for his workers and their families.

So while some of these treatments can co-exist, it would be unusual to introduce several simultaneously. Choices have to be made between these and a long list of other possible 'treatments' if an organization's problems are to be resolved. Our concern is that they are sometimes applied inappropriately. Not only will this have been wasteful and disruptive but, more seriously, it will have diverted effort and attention from the treatment that could have given the greatest benefit at that moment in time.

More recently there has been a spate of books that analyse apparently successful companies and put forward what the author sees as the reasons for their success for other managers to emulate. These companies are seen to have 'excellence', 'built to last', and who have moved from 'being good to great'. Such books are very popular and the 'treatments' they put forward become very 'fashionable'. They are another example of the attractiveness of a 'quick fix' that are taken up by organizations that do not want to spend the time and effort on the thorough approach to diagnosis that is advocated in the following chapters of this book.

More worryingly there have been, in more recent times, consultants putting forward, with a great deal of marketing hype, 'instruments' and training packages that purport to be able to do great things for organizations, the latest example being 'neuroleadership', said to be based on developments in neuroscience. But anyone can set themselves up as an expert in this area, and then convince managers to use their personal interpretation of neuroscience as a way of developing people or bringing about organizational change. The use of such panaceas distracts managers from what they should really be doing, as set out later in the book, to solve their immediate problems and add to organizational fitness.

Then there are the TV programmes where a management 'guru' studies an ailing company or organization and then puts forward proposals to make it better. Those featured have included John Harvey-Jones on industrial organizations, Gerry Robinson on National Health Service hospitals, Mary Portas on shops, Alex Polizzi on family firms and Gordon Ramsey on restaurants. They do it by collecting information through interviews and observation, analysed in the light of their considerable personal experience and by well-honed intuition, to produce a 'treatment' for the organization to make it fit again. They did not always succeed! Again, well-meaning and entertaining as these programmes are the editing of them can mislead the viewers to think that diagnosis that leads to an appropriate and lasting treatment is easy as long as the diagnostician has the standing, confidence and charisma to get their solutions accepted. They are useful in awakening the need to search for a treatment for an ailing organization, but are not helpful in indicating how it should be done. The purpose of this book is to make suggestions as to how an organization can develop its own tailor-made solution to become fitter.

Sometimes organizations require severe treatment. In clinical psychology the so-called 'last resort' treatment is pre-frontal leucotomy, equivalent in organizational terms to sacking the chief executive. On the other hand, one chief executive, Jack Welch, was famous (if not notorious) for ordering an annual cull of 10 per cent of the management in General Electric, this would appear to be a modern equivalent of the process of decimation that was said to take place in Roman legions.

Then there are those severe kinds of mental illness which require placing the patient in an institution to be cared for both for their own safety and that of the community. The history of mental hospitals is a chequered one but they do not have to be like the infamous Bedlam hospital in South London. Again, it is the diagnosis to determine who really needs to be placed in an institution which is crucial, then how the institution is to be run, the flexibility of the treatments and the amount of control over the patients being the key issues. After 600 years of structural and behavioural changes Bedlam has been transformed into the much acclaimed Bethlem Royal Hospital.

Recent trends in the UK have been towards closing mental hospitals and putting mentally ill people out to 'cope in the community', leaving social forces to play their part in their treatment. It has been argued that this approach is more efficient and cost effective for the community and more pleasant for the patient, on the other hand, some people are now very concerned that this trend has gone too far and that there is not enough residential accommodation for those who are in acute phases of their illnesses.

In organizational life all this can be mirrored in the adoption of the policies of nationalization and privatization. Following the Second World War, it was thought that there was too much risk to society to allow the key functions of a state, such as energy, transport and water, to be controlled by private hands. The cure was 'nationalization'. So great institutions of state were established to run these services and utilities. But, as in the history of mental hospitals, the patients (organizations) became institutionalized, expensive to run, starved of adequate resources, inefficient, sluggish and inflexible, aggravated by the paucity of training in how to run a business that was given to the senior civil servants assigned to direct these organizations.

Some then saw 'privatization' as being the 'cure' for these problems and their thinking may have been influenced by the benefits to the Exchequer of possible reductions in subsidies and/or the potential income from franchises and sales of shares. Accordingly, the organizations were put out to the community (sold to shareholders) and 'market forces' were allowed to work with the treatment to make them cost-effective and efficient. There was still seen the need to have some kind of institutional control through 'regulators', but this was applied loosely and at a distance.

Now, in some areas, the pendulum is starting to swing back towards tighter institutional control, to handle some of the self-indulgences and personal excesses, delusions of grandeur and sheer greed of 'sick' organizations that are given too much freedom when they are lacking the power of self-control, aggravated by the lack of training in and adherence to business ethics given to the directors of those organizations. The banks are a sad example.

So the key problems of severe individual and organizational health remain. Just how much institutional control is required to balance the freedom to be dangerous to oneself or society?

The Classification of Treatments

The history of 'organizational treatments' reflects the treatments developed for mentally ill people. Mental illness can be grouped into two main kinds, the psychoses and the neuroses. The psychoses are mainly due to structural and chemical malfunction of the brain and are treated with drugs and, in severe cases, with electric shock, cauterization and surgery. The neuroses arise from behavioural malfunction and are treated by a wide range of 'talking cures' and in minor cases with 'counselling'. A great scandal in the treatment of mental illness has been the treatment of behavioural problems with structural treatments and structural problems with behavioural treatments.

So too with organizational treatments, treating a sick organization with 'behavioural' treatments when what is needed is some re-structuring (that is, changing the way that responsibilities are divided and power is shared) is a great waste of money and time. Likewise for those organizations with behavioural problems, for example inept management and poor interpersonal relations, re-structuring them can cause untold misery. The National Health Service is a sad example of this. So we first offer a classification of treatments based on whether they are aimed at 'structure' or 'behaviour'.

Looking back over the recent history of management, 'organizational treatments' can be scaled and grouped according to how invasive, disruptive, expensive and severe they are to the organization. We classify the largest changes as being 'mega', that is, 'great' in terms of cost and disruption, through 'macro' (large), 'midi' (middling), 'mini' (small) and 'micro' (very small), gentle and with little disruption and cost.

STRUCTURAL

Applying Values and Beliefs About People and Organizations – 'Mega' Approaches

Politicians, social philosophers and others form views about the kinds of organization that are most desirable. For some the financial success of the organization and its owners/shareholders is paramount, while others will focus on meeting the needs of customers/users or on the rewards and working conditions of employees.

Values and beliefs form the basis of the preferred treatments of governments and the multinational firms of consultants. Implementation often involves structural change in the organization, always very expensive, sometimes very disruptive and painful for employees at all levels who may be made redundant from one internal organization with no guarantee of employment in the organization that replaces it. Such 'treatments' include:

Nationalization and *privatization* are treatments much favoured by politicians of all flavours, particularly those at the extremes of their parties. They can be seen to be used in times of crisis. They invariably involve drawing up and passing new Acts of Parliament and are hotly debated, especially by the press and media. Their support, one way or the other, by delegates at party conferences is expressed with great vehemence.

Worker participation, worker control and *co-ownership* are treatments much favoured by 'left leaning' commentators. They were used to great positive effect in post-war West Germany with worker committees and worker board members. Along with trading light bulbs it was the cornerstone of the survival and success of the Volkswagen car company. Support for these ideas is often urged on various sociological networks, by those searching for utopian societies or just simple cooperatives.

Business process re-engineering (BPR) seeks to help companies restructure their organizations through basically rethinking and radically redesigning the use of the organization's existing resources. Such an approach, which is likely to result in 'downsizing' the number of employees, appears to be favoured by academics and consultants with mathematical/engineering backgrounds.

Imposing Systems of Management – 'Macro' Approaches

Systems of management tend to be preferred 'treatments' of the smaller consultancy firms and of HR directors. They can be quick, but costly and can have an immediate impact. They can also be quite disruptive of everyday working life. They would appear to apply more to improving organizational fitness rather than as a 'cure' for a major illness, they include:

Work study, management by objectives, target setting and job design: these approaches tend to involve experts studying the work, working out the best ways of doing it and then telling employees what to do.

Job rotation and job enrichment: adoption of some of these approaches may mean that employees are involved in the design of the work, in theory, more variety can give greater interest in the work to be done and provide a more flexible workforce; in practice, some may prefer to specialize in just one kind of work, while others may take the view that greater flexibility should be rewarded by higher pay.

Merit rating, payment by results and bonuses: essentially the view is that productivity will increase if it affects pay; the two main dangers are: (a) that targets will be achieved too easily and (b) that quality will suffer. A plethora of motivational theories underpin these treatments, which have been both a source of benefit and unhappiness for employees.

Total Quality Management: TQM involves the review of an organization's processes against pre-determined lists of activities and functions. It is formally defined as a 'management philosophy and company practices that aim to harness the human and material resources of an organization in the most effective way to achieve the objectives of the organization'.

Advocates of TQM say that by recording and reviewing processes, organizations can make significant improvement. Critics say that the approach is time-consuming and does not attempt to assess the quality of the reviewing processes; for this reason the potential impact and benefits of the approach may vary greatly from one organization to the next.

At the transition point along the multidimensional scale of disruptiveness, cost, severity and acceptability is the scheme sponsored by the UK government, Investors in People. Investors in People encourages training by auditing the instruction and other training given to employees and giving recognition to organizations which can demonstrate that effective training has been given to all its employees. Because effective employee training can benefit the employees themselves, the users/customers and the owners/shareholders, it is far less contentious than some of the other approaches based on values and beliefs.

BEHAVIOURAL

Applying Techniques for Describing, Assessing and Changing Behaviour – 'Midi' Approaches

There is a deep conflict within these 'treatments', between those that are development oriented and those that are based on assessment and this dichotomy is also present in the approaches to organizational fitness that we describe in Chapter 7. This conflict of approach can probably be traced back to the scientific training of the advocates. 'Hard' science training, such as in physics and chemistry, has probably left the view that to change something one has to first measure it, apply the 'treatment' and then re-measure to display that change has been successful. This is fine for inanimate/physical objects that do not object to being measured, but can be disastrous for thinking/feeling people who could have a severe negative reaction to being 'measured', particularly when the measurements are irrelevant and inept. 'Soft science' training, such as in psychology and sociology, probably leads to the view that things can be changed without first measuring anything. This observation is particularly relevant to all the various approaches taken to performance management across organizations.

Performance Appraisal, Performance Management, Managerial Styles and Grids, 360° Feedback

One way of improving performance is for line managers to analyse the work done, along with the member of staff, as part of a staff appraisal programme and then to offer feedback and suggest ways of improving it. However, some managers lack the expertise to do this, particularly with employees who lack self-awareness or who are resistant to change. So psychologists and others have devised techniques to help describe, assess and change behaviour. They can be used both by those who need to address problems, and those who want to take their skills to a higher level. Unfortunately these processes are easier described than carried out. Organizations frequently underestimate the amount of training and commitment that is required to inculcate the interpersonal skills needed to do this well. Instead they design and impose a plethora of appraisal forms, full of rating scales and boxes to tick, in the vain hope that by having them filled out once a year on each employee they would somehow improve work performance and job satisfaction. Many set up 'rating exercises' in the hope that this will reduce the amount of subjectivity and often prejudice and bias, that are prevalent in such ratings-based appraisal schemes. Hence the existence of so much disrepute surrounding staff appraisal and performance management.

Inculcating Skills in the Job, 'Mini' Approaches – Supervisory and Leadership Skills, Through Coaching and Counselling

Studies have identified skills which are required in most supervisory posts and it is generally felt that supervisors should be trained in these skills before they take up their first line-management post. Such training goes back a long way. In the aftermath of the Second World War 'Training Within Industry' (TWI) was imported from the United States by the government of the time and expanded into an industry in itself. It had a great beneficial effect and has left a powerful legacy of supervisor training. Its principles were carried forward by the Industrial Society (renamed the Work Foundation in 2002). Such training helped to boost the confidence of supervisors and, through the safety programme, helped to prevent many industrial accidents. It took a while for some organizations to realise that all levels of management need training in leadership skills, while others still do not realise that. We discuss leadership training in Chapter 8.

Displaying Good Intentions Towards the Staff – 'Micro' Approaches

These are the least disruptive, cheapest (except for worker welfare schemes) and most gentle of all the treatments available to organizations. They can be traced back to Robert Owen's model village of New Lanark in Scotland in the 1810s, to Titus Salt's model village of Saltaire in Bradford in the 1880s and in particular to australian psychiatrist Elton Mayo's efforts to improve working conditions in textile mills in Pittsburgh in the 1920s and at the Hawthorne telecommunications factory in Chicago in the 1930s. They were much embraced by the great British Quaker chocolate companies in the twentieth century. They can be surrounded by cynicism but when the 'good intentions' are sincere they can have a deep and long-lasting beneficial effect on an organization.

Concern for people, winning friends and influencing people, transactional analysis, engaging, empowering, one-minute managing, management-by-walking about, exhortations for excellence, threats to survival, charismatic leadership.

All these treatments involve face-to-face interaction between managers and their staff. They come naturally to managers who possess that elusive trait of 'charisma', but are difficult for the less outward going and socially confident. The essence of them has recently been distilled into the current fashionable concept of employee engagement. This would appear to involve managers asking their staff open questions, such as 'How do you think your job should be done?' Then following it with a gentle probe, such as, 'What do you think would be the difficulty in doing it that way?' Then, above all, actively listening to and analysing the answers. Many are based on the Skinnerian technology of 'reinforcement' where praise is seen as a powerful reward and chastisement seen as having a negative influence on behaviour. They have frequently been dismissed as 'soft' and as 'gimmicks' and have had a bad press from some cynical commentators about management. They are easier said than done. To some managers this way of doing their job comes easily to them. Somehow, by the way they speak, look and conduct themselves they are 'warmed to' by their staff. To other managers, direct interaction with their staff is found difficult and distasteful. To others there is a disliked whiff of manipulation and even exploitation surrounding direct interaction with staff. As will be further elaborated in Chapter 8 all these interactions require considerable interpersonal skills. It is these skills that are at the core of 'leadership' and are at the centre of bringing about change in the behaviour of individuals and the health of an organization.

Concluding Comments

History shows that all the above treatments have worked at one time or another and that is why they continue to be applied. When used skilfully and appropriately they can certainly improve organizational fitness. How well they have cured deep organizational ills is not immediately apparent. Also, whether a different treatment at that time would have been better, is not known. There are many, sad, examples of people who have searched for fitness and longevity by jogging but who have died prematurely because of the effect of the exercise on medical conditions that had not been diagnosed. Similarly, there are many examples of otherwise healthy organizations going out of business because of a lack of financial support. So our plea is that the implementation of a drastic and expensive 'cure' without a thorough diagnosis taking place is indefensible and likely to do more harm than good.

However, in the meantime, a practical implication of the above analysis of the various treatments used by organizations to improve the health and productivity of the organization is to start at the bottom of the above taxonomy, with those treatments that are the least disruptive, least expensive and most gentle. Then to wait and see what impact they would have on organizational fitness. Many a senior manager would be surprised just how quick and powerful such low level 'treatments' can be when applied skilfully. The famous 'Hawthorne investigations' at the Western Electric works in Chicago in the early 1930s, referred to earlier, showed that just talking with the staff about their work made a large impact on their morale and productivity. This has now been packaged into the process called 'engagement', and is gaining popularity as a way to create a great place to work. Despite all the current publicity it is still basically showing concern to the staff of an organization by asking them open questions about what they think of their jobs, listening to the answers and, wherever feasible, making changes in the light of what the staff have said. Perhaps just by facing up to the fact that the organization could be fitter and more healthy would have a beneficial effect, then setting up a process for bringing it about is in itself the start of treatment. This initial, gentle and cheap approach could pave the way for gaining acceptance of the major 'cure' once a comprehensive diagnostic effort has taken place that makes use of the analysis and the suggestions made in the following chapters.

Chapter 3
Describing and Understanding How Organizations Work

This chapter offers models to help describe organizations and explain how they work. It will take a 'systems' approach, using a 'closed' systems model to explain how many medium-to-large organizations work within the context of a state. Then it takes an 'open' systems approach to explaining how many medium-to-large work organizations transform their resources into goods, services and job satisfaction. Small organizations are laws unto themselves!

Before something can be fixed we need to have some understanding of how it works and how it should appear when it is working properly. In broad terms the better our understanding, the faster will be our successful diagnosis of what is wrong. Can mechanics diagnose problems and repair engines unless they know how an engine works? Can medical doctors cure an illness without understanding how a body works? Can an electronics engineer fix a computer without at least understanding what the components do and how to test whether they are working?

Analogies are blurred by the trend towards the de-skilling of trouble-shooting and fault-finding, so that diagnosis sometimes becomes a matter of fitting a replacement part to see if it works and the faulty part is simply thrown away rather than repaired. A do-it-yourselfer can get lucky and hit upon, sometimes literally, a fault in a piece of equipment and put it right, but anything complicated and they are stumped. The equivalent in organizations is to sack the person who appears responsible for a malfunction and bear the brunt of an unfair dismissal claim.

The fringes of the world of work are populated by managers, consultants, academics and even 'gurus' who, for a fee, will study and write a report on an organization, suggesting, sometimes very radical, changes. Their understanding of how organizations work more often than not is just based on their personal experiences. By intuition and good fortune they may well propose some recommendations that are beneficial to the organization, but sadly, they often miss the crucial issues and the changes they recommend cause misery and mayhem throughout the organization. What if medical consultants went about their business that way, only basing their treatments on their own personal experiences, the suffering that would cause!

However, there is some excuse for the current state of affairs, the research and literature on how organizations work is remarkably sparse. The chapters in organizational analysis texts are mainly descriptive of organizational structures and how decisions get made and the constraints on organizational change. Even though there are shelves in business school libraries laden with books on management and organizational behaviour, there is very little in them on how organizations actually work. There is a great deal of high level abstract concepts on organizational theory but somehow putting into simple words what actually happens in an effective work organization seems to be lacking. The syllabi for students who wish to become car mechanics, computer engineers, medical doctors and for most of the other practical professions start with a considerable allocation of teaching time on how the object of their study actually works. Not so in the business and management schools where the focus for first-year students is invariably on the context in which work organizations exist or on the basic techniques for running them.

The Diversity of Organizations

It is likely that the extreme diversity of organizations also contributes to the lack of progress. Work organizations clearly differ in a number of ways including:

- Their size.

- Their ownership.

- Their objectives, e.g. profit-making, not for profit, charities.

- The people that they employ, e.g. nationality and culture, abilities, personality and needs.

- The technologies that they use and whether any production comprises unique items, small batches, large batches or continuous production.

- Their structures, e.g. how work is done and the way that responsibilities are divided.

- The extent to which they subcontract and outsource; this may include key functions such as personnel and finance.

The machines of life, including all the species in the diverse animal kingdom as well as the human body, can be described by focusing on the systems that they have in common, such as the cardiovascular system, the gastroenterological system, the reproductive system etc. Ultimately all these systems are 'open systems' in the sense that there is interaction between them and the environment in which the animal or person is living. So too are many systems common to all work organizations, particularly those which make extensive use of sub-contracting and outsourcing.

Elsewhere in this book we comment on what can be learned about diagnosis and treatment from other professions, particularly medical doctors. In considering this chapter we suggest that an even better analogy might be that of the work of veterinary surgeons who aim to diagnose and treat a very wide range of animals. All animals have respiratory systems to enable them to get oxygen into their bodies, but how they do it varies greatly. In practice the diversity of animals means that veterinary surgeons do tend to specialize, either in terms of the animals (e.g. horses, farm animals or small domestic pets) or in terms of illnesses such as cancer. Indeed, it will be observed that those who advise organizations also tend to specialize in terms of industry/technology or sector (such as government, health, retailing, or charities).

The World of Work and Management

When approaching the fiendish problem of explaining how organizations work the first thing to do is to place work organizations into their context and to identify the sources of influence on their activity. At this stage our comments relate to medium to large organizations, perhaps employing upwards of 50 people and not making use of subcontracting or outsourcing.

Figure 3.1 indicates three levels that need to be understood and managed and if mismanaged can be a severe cause of organization malfunction. Organizations do not, of course, manage themselves, so the model indicates eight groups of managers that are involved in ensuring that the whole system works well. If any group or individual is inept then again malfunction will

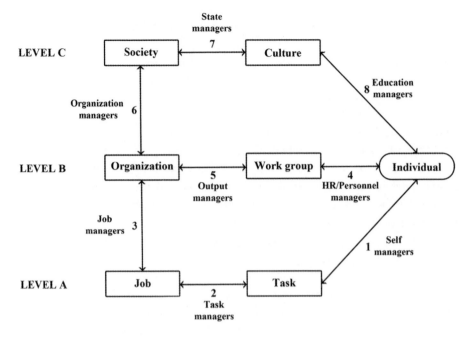

Figure 3.1   The world of work and management

occur. Because the boundaries of this system are very wide and all components interact, it can be regarded as a 'closed' system.

The most influential managers are at Level C, the State Managers, Politicians and Civil Servants. Their actions, decisions and skills, or lack of them, have a profound effect on work organizations. Managers at this level set the taxation policy of the country and establish how well it is applied through all sizes of organizations and kinds of work. When they get their decisions and legislation wrong the whole economic, legal and education systems within which organizations operate will suffer. Then they have the responsibility to listen to and protect 'whistle-blowers' and, when required, set up formal inquiries into failing organizations.

At Level B are the Education Managers, Vice-chancellors, Heads of Schools and Colleges, Teachers, Administrators and Organization Managers such as CEOs, Directors and Senior Managers. The Education Managers are responsible for transmitting and shaping our culture and educating and training the work force, at all levels. Again, there can be very serious consequences to the health of work organizations if they fall down on their task. The balance between producing widely educated, free thinking adults and vocationally trained specialists is a very hard one to achieve. The Organization Managers are responsible for setting up and running organizations. They have great scope for inadequacy as recent events in our society and some of our commercial organizations have shown. They are a considerable source of organizational malfunctioning. They have the responsibility and power to authorize diagnoses and appoint external consultants. They also have the responsibility to own up when they have made a mess of things, not an infrequent occurrence!

Level A is where all the day-to-day activities of organizational life take place. The Output Managers are responsible for how work is planned, responsibilities allocated, orders met and policies carried out. They are in a good position to pick up and report signals of malfunctioning. They can have a key influence on to what extent staff feel 'engaged'. The HR/Personnel Managers are responsible for the recruiting, training and developing of the work force. Then they can check how well an organization is working by keeping and reviewing records of performance, turnover and sickness, some of the key indicators of organizational well-being. They are in a key position for getting detailed information on organizational health by conducting probing interviews with staff that are leaving. The Job Managers are in charge of organizing how the work is to be done, and who should do it. Getting the expectations of the organization and the individual workers in balance is a crucial part of their job. The Task Managers, supervisors and foremen, make sure that what needs to be done is done. How they go about this underpins just how well staff 'feel' about their jobs. Finally, individuals are responsible for managing themselves, how hard and effectively they work and behave. They can decide to be collaborative or oppose a diagnostic investigation or an application of a treatment.

When organizations are not functioning as they should the reason why can be traced to any one of the eight groups of managers identified in Figure 3.1. Considering whether one of these groups is the main source of malfunction is one of the objectives of *diagnosis*, to be discussed in Chapter 5.

An Open System for Analysing Behaviour at Work

In simple terms and starting with a minimalist view, work organizations can be conceived as a series of 'open systems'. They take in resources such as people, materials, equipment, capital and transform this 'input' into goods and services of various kinds and wealth, disposable money and, if it is healthy, job satisfaction and even joy, for its members.

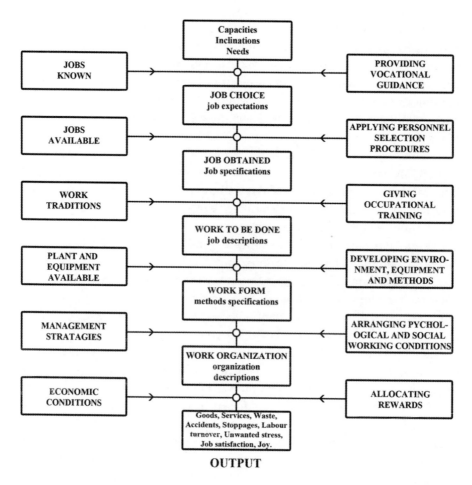

Figure 3.2   An open system for analysing behaviour at work

Clearly some organizational systems concern finance, information technology, sales etc. This book concentrates on the organizational systems that involve people. At best the systems will enable people to develop their potential and reward them with a good standard of living. At worst they may leave people mentally and physically exhausted or even injured or dead. A series of processes which involve and affect people are shown above in Figure 3.2.

Figure 3.2 is a model of a series of processes involving people, it is not a flow diagram. Its structure makes the point that a work organization is not a single closed system that exists isolated from its environment, but a series of linked open processes that are very much influenced by each other and everything around them, such as the quality of people outputted from the educational system, the supply of capital from the financial system and the availability of raw materials. When an organization is studied in order to diagnose problems or improve fitness, it can be important to understand the relationship between these processes and the way that responsibilities are divided between staff, there may be times when processes are not in place and other times when responsibilities for processes overlap or are even duplicated.

This model can be regarded as depicting a 'manufacturing engine of people at work'. The power of the engine is provided by people entering at the top of the model, the 'raw materials' come in through the processes down the spine of the model, the mechanics are provided by the processes on the left, and the tuning and maintenance come from the techniques on the right of the model. If all these activities are balanced and well-managed 'motivation' is generated, akin to oil in an engine and the 'output' of the whole working system can be seen at the bottom of the model. The range of outputs is of course far wider than can be set out in the box. For this output to be achieved the system needs to be 'managed' and this is done by the various kinds of managers set out in Figure 3.1.

For some, Figure 3.1 will raise the question as to what makes a 'manager' a 'leader'. This is controversial ground. For some the difference is simply one the numbers of staff directly managed or influenced – leaders must have followers! Others consider status, leaders being the managers at the top of an organization or having a senior position in society (i.e. Level C in Figure 3.1). Other focus on objectives and intent, suggesting that managers aim to maintain the 'status quo' while leaders aim to transform the way that things are done; viewed in this way, the manager of a small team at Level 3 could be seen to be a successful leader. For others it is a simply a matter whether objectives were achieved, while yet another approach is to consider not only the amount of change required and the success with which objectives were achieved, but also the extent to which the results benefitted the organization and the society in which it operates. These contrasting views highlight the potential differences in what can be required of managers. However, what successful managers have in common are the abilities to diagnose what should be done or changed next in order to resolve problems or improve fitness.

The external factors surrounding an organization can be very severe as organizations do not exist in a perfect world, they have to work under many constraints. These constraints are listed within the boxes on the left of the model and can have a very debilitating effect on the 'engine of work' if they are lacking or inappropriate.

Organizational starvation occurs when it is deprived of sufficient resources, for example people, equipment and investment, as with all starvation it is a slow debilitating process that eventually takes its toll. Organizational anorexia is when an organization downsizes itself beyond need or even reason. If the organization is starved of investment resources, or has a poor product, gets its markets invaded, or even just has outdated equipment, it will get sick.

At the top of the figure our approach starts with what is inside people, their different types and levels of capacity for different types and levels of work. Their differing inclinations towards the satisfactions that work can provide and their needs, for wealth, security, power, excitement and all the other components of life, the driving force of organizational activity. All these are determined by an individual's background, up-bringing and their education.

Down the central spine of the model are the structural components of the organization. They can be termed the *constants* as they are mainly fixed by the conventions, precedents and standard practices and techniques of organizational management. They make up all work organizations, to be productive and healthy each of these *constants* has to be appropriate and work. If not they can be a source of considerable organizational sickness, but they can be changed, often with great difficulty.

The following examples from the model illustrates the working of each of the *constants* and the concepts and techniques that underpin them and the kinds of organizational practices that can cause problems through inadequate attention being given to them.

In a free society people can choose whether they work, what work to do and who they work for. They do this on the basis of the jobs they know about and the expectations they have about their work and whether a particular organization will meet the more important of them. If nobody wants to work for the organization, or if the incumbents go on strike the organization is certainly chronically, if not terminally, sick. So there is a great deal that an organization can do to attract people to them and also many mistakes they can make. Some large organizations frequently put out the image, their so-called 'Employer Brand', in their recruitment literature that they are great places to work in with 'varied work', 'travel opportunities', 'good promotion prospects', but in reality those who are recruited can find that they are rigid in all these areas. Disappointment and dissatisfaction soon results, 'one learns in school of tribulation the folly of one's expectation'!

The concepts and techniques of Vocational Guidance have evolved in recent decades and can help individuals and organizations with the process of job and career choice. Governments and local authorities around the world have set up facilities to aid the process, although whether they are sufficiently well resourced is often a moot point. The same comment can be made about the numbers of staff and other resources allocated by schools, colleges and universities to students independent advice on their job and career choices. Work organizations are well-advised to work closely with these specialists, not least because most teachers are happy to talk about the progress of their students and this can be a useful source of able recruits.

That said, recruiting only the most able recruits can itself lead to problems. Although it may be conventional to require specific qualifications for particular jobs, it is sometimes the case that the work to be done does not really need people with that level or type of qualification. Not only does the organization find recruitment difficult but those appointed will soon become dissatisfied and even bitter and twisted and a pain to all around them.

Indeed a variation of this problem occurred in one organization which recruited apprentices. Tradition was that the small number of apprentices achieving distinction would be offered further professional training. However, some apprentices did not complete their training and aptitude tests were introduced with the aim of reducing the numbers who 'dropped out'. It was found that the aptitude tests were successful in reducing the number of drop-outs, but their introduction also meant an increase in the numbers achieving distinction. The employer was unable to offer the further training to all who reached distinction and ill-will followed.

A person then has to be chosen for a job and this depends on the competition for the jobs that are available and the personnel selection process of the employing organization. Invariably some kind of training will be required. There are many traditions, conventions and even laws that bear upon the ways organizations go about training their staff. The work then needs to be done. The availability of plant, equipment and the appropriate technology come into play here along with the techniques of work study and ergonomics.

Work is carried out in a social environment and how people are managed and the facilities they have surrounding their work are involved here. Findings from attitude surveys repeatedly identify the importance of communications and if people are to be fully engaged and effective they need to understand what the organization is trying to achieve and the part that they can play in its success.

However, it is also clear that people vary greatly in their expectations of work and indeed of life. Some see work as an opportunity to develop and learn, to achieve promotion and ultimately a better lifestyle. Others see work merely as a source of income, while others view it as a source of exploitation.

Finally in this model of how organizations work the tricky question of the allocation of rewards, both financial and non-financial, has to be addressed. If the general economic conditions are favourable then this need not be too difficult, if they are poor then this issue in organizational activity can be a tough one.

Other Organizations

At the start of this chapter we referred to the many ways in which organizations can differ, including their size.

Many apparently large organizations are not what they appear to be. Many fast food outlets trading under well-known brand names are in fact a series of privately-owned franchises, while those who run British sub-post offices are self-employed, as are General Practitioners working for the National Health Service. Publishers do not employ their authors. We could go on!

On the other hand, some small organizations can have many of the features and functions of conventional large organizations, with some employees covering a wide range of functions. But other smaller organizations tend to operate in specialist fields, sometimes contracting out many aspects of their work including accountancy and book-keeping, information technology, recruitment and employment law, and so on.

Indeed, some organizations have been described as 'virtual organizations' because they comprise just a few staff with all the organization's activities 'contracted out' including purchasing and manufacturing, sales and marketing, and accountancy and book-keeping.

In turn this means that some employees and self-employed people can have work with distinctive features. For example, some are able to work at home, making extensive use of computer and phone facilities, while others may travel extensively as sales people, representatives or agents. If employed by others, both groups may have very little contact with their line management.

Whatever the size or structure of an organization, there is no reason why it should not be assessed and reviewed to identify potential problems and to improve its fitness. But clearly those making the assessment need to spend time understanding how the organization is supposed to work before making recommendations for improvement and such a review may need to include services that are contracted out or even franchised. Further, the options for improvement may be limited by the location and working life-style of the staff involved.

Concluding Comments

Figures 3.1 and 3.2 have set out the processes that are needed to be identified, described and taken into account in organizational diagnosis and treatment. It is our view that if all the processes are appropriate to an organization and working well both individually and together, the organization should be functioning well, meeting its objectives, being productive, providing a satisfying working environment for its employees and even having standing in its community and with the financial institutions.

But if one or more of the components are failing and causing the organization to slow or break down in its delivery of 'output' the organization will be seen to be on the way to being regarded as 'sick'.

Thus these and other models may be able to contribute to Organizational Diagnosis in practice and we hope that the proposed systems will lay a foundation for others to build on. However, whether and in what ways they can be used in practice is one of the issues discussed in the next chapter.

Chapter 4

Preparing to Diagnose and Manage Problems

This is the first of three chapters dealing with Organizational Diagnosis and Management. Together they are about examining, diagnosing, managing and monitoring *problems* which are adversely affecting organizational health, and how to plan and staff these activities. We advise that all three chapters should be read before any diagnostic work is planned.

Problem Indicators

Measures that may indicate problems are of four possible kinds. They are measures of *behaviour* at work, of *performance* at work, of the attributes of employees, and of how people feel about their work.

MEASURES OF BEHAVIOUR AT WORK

Measures such as attendance, timekeeping, hours of overtime worked, labour turnover and time lost due to walk-outs and other industrial action can be calculated in different ways but are relatively objective. So if trends are being monitored over time and the methods of calculation have not been changed, there can be signs of an organization improving (or getting worse) from the point of view of the people working in it.

However, any comparison between organizations will be misleading unless made on a 'like for like' basis. For example, some organizations will include the long-term sick in departmental calculations of absence figures, others will not. Further, important trends may not be apparent from summary statistics, as when overall labour turnover figures are low, but masking high turnover among young people.

Whether or not the measures cause questions to be asked or trigger a request for an urgent investigation will depend not only on the actual figures but on local circumstances and the expectations of managers. Relatively high turnover may be tolerated if there is a ready supply of applicants who can quickly reach required standards. In contrast, a long period of low turnover might be investigated because it could be a sign of complacency and of a failure to attract those with new ideas.

MEASURES OF PERFORMANCE AT WORK

These include such indices as number of items made, sold, repaired and stored. They can appear to be objective, and are often used to assess the performance of individuals or groups, but experienced managers will know that even if the measures are consistent they may be misleading.

Sometimes errors arise because of confusion – as when the products are found to be faulty at the end of a production line, immediately repaired, and then replaced on the production line so that they are counted twice! And again, differences in calculation can mislead. For example, some vehicle manufacturers report only the numbers that they employ and ignore those employed by their suppliers. On this basis Volkswagen, currently the most profitable vehicle manufacturer, appears to be among the least efficient.

Again there can be different interpretations of figures. If the sales figures of an individual have dropped, one supervisor might acknowledge that products have been found unreliable or even unsafe, or perhaps reflect the impact of new competition. But another supervisor might dismiss these factors and attribute the poor sales to a salesman's lack of effort or ability.

ASSESSMENT OF THE ATTRIBUTES OF EMPLOYEES

Many organizations update information about the knowledge, skills and abilities of their employees, including assessments made by supervisors and managers as part of an appraisal scheme. Such assessments are widely used – they can affect pay and promotion decisions and the planning of training and development and can even be used to check on the effectiveness of selection procedures. But while some are based on the relatively objective measures of behaviour and performance described earlier, they may be unduly influenced by opinion and casual observation and become misleading. Rating scales used in appraisal and performance management schemes are particularly questionable if those making the ratings have not been trained.

Whatever the results of formal assessments, it is the reputation of some individuals that can affect views formed about them. Once a CEO has formed a view about an individual – perhaps based on a brief meeting during a time of success or crisis, others may go along with that view rather than with evidence systematically collected from other sources.

HOW PEOPLE FEEL ABOUT THEIR WORK

Examples of indicators of how people feel about their work are shown in Appendix A and can be assessed in two ways, first by observation and second by seeking the views of employees. Observations are a somewhat rough and ready method and, if brief, there is also the question as to whether what was observed was typical. That said, impressions gained by experienced managers may be one of the early signs that things are not well. Information can be sought from employees in a variety of ways including individual interviews, focus groups and questionnaires.

A special source of information is that which comes from 'whistle-blowers'. Although only a small group or even just a single individual may be involved, the allegations made may be very important. Because of the different kinds of reasons that may motivate a whistle-blower much care needs to be taken when interpreting and using this information. However it can be a useful trigger and signal as to whether a diagnostic investigation is needed and where it might be started.

More about these methods and the interpretation of findings will be said later in this book.

Ways of Diagnosing Problems

At present there seem to be two main approaches to the systematic diagnosis problems. The first is to identify any departures from good practice. The second is to look back over time to see if there were times when things were better – or even worse – and to look for associated changes that may explain the variations. The two approaches are not mutually exclusive, and experience suggests that it will it often be the case that 'multiple causes are having multiple effects'. We outline other approaches in Chapter 10.

An example of the first approach concerns a comprehensive school unable to attract teachers in spite of having a new, enthusiastic head teacher, stable staff, good buildings and other facilities, and a catchment area containing both private and public housing. The Local Authority administering the school had placed a small advertisement in a national publication advertising many teaching jobs. The Local Authority was infamous for its poor performance in 'league tables' of results, and the advertisement said little more than 'Teachers Wanted, apply to the Head Teacher'. No attempt had been made to explain the many attractive features of the particular school. When that was done in a redesigned advertisement, there was a dramatic increase in the number of applicants and all the vacancies were filled.

Examples of the second approach are given in subsequent chapters. They show how problems such as high labour turnover can be traced to specific departments in an organization and sometimes to specific changes in the work or working conditions.

Arguably the best way of describing how to do something is to demonstrate or observe it. But the cognitive and other processes involved in organizational diagnosis and management are rarely observed or recorded. So next we discuss the challenge of describing the whole process, before suggesting questions that can facilitate the preparation and examination stages.

The Challenge of Describing the Whole Process

At the heart of the whole process is the term 'diagnosis' which is often associated with medical doctors. What can we learn from them?

Doctors often start a consultation with a phrase like 'What brings you here today?' and you respond. What happens next depends on what you say. It also depends on your age and your medical history. You will probably be asked a series of further questions and may even be examined.

Whether a doctor or patient it may be difficult to predict the time required for diagnosis until an initial exchange of information has taken place. That said, doctors can normally make the better predictions because many conditions are associated with a patient's age and their previous medical history.

Account needs to be taken of the views of 'patients'. Unless we have confidence that our medical doctor has appreciated our symptoms and our concerns, we may not accept the diagnosis or persevere with the treatment. And if the treatment is too unpleasant or demanding we may decide to stop making ourselves ill.

In our view there is no agreed approach to preparation for organizational diagnosis and the underlying processes are rarely discussed. But there seem to us to be some similarities with medical diagnosis – that the stages of preparation, diagnosis and treatment can overlap, and that the preparatory stages may need to be revisited in the light of emerging information. Indeed, in our view the four stages of (i) preparation and examination, (ii) diagnosis, (iii) management, and (iv) monitoring, form an iterative cycle of activities which may need to be repeated until the problem is resolved. In the early cycles diagnosis may not be possible and the management and monitoring stages may both involve the collection of further information, diagnosis and treatment may not be possible until several cycles have taken place.

Questions to Inform Diagnosis and Management

Information that will form the basis of diagnosis, management and perhaps treatment of problems can be gathered by means of the following questions.

WHAT IS THE PRESENTING PROBLEM? HAVE THE SYMPTOMS BEEN VERIFIED?

'Presenting problem' means not only the problem that has led to the view that 'something needs to be done', but also related information such as when the problem first occurred, and which parts of the organization are/are not affected by it. It can be important to verify the 'presenting problem' and associated information. For example, as described earlier, an organization may appear to employ excessive numbers of staff simply because it manufactures all the components that it requires and does not sub-contract work elsewhere.

As well as verifying the accuracy of the information collected and any calculations made, the interpretation of the data should be verified too. After all it is a matter interpretation and judgement as to whether labour turnover is 'acceptable' or 'potentially disastrous' and circumstances need to be considered as well as the actual figures.

WHAT ARE THE CURRENT AND POTENTIAL IMPACTS OF THE PROBLEM?

What impact is this problem having both directly and indirectly? For example, the failure to complete work on time would be a direct result of an inability to recruit and/or retain staff. An indirect result may be that the missed targets are adversely affecting the organization's reputation, and that further orders and potential new customers are being lost. There is also the matter of whether this is a 'one-off' problem or part of a series of related incidents.

So that organizations can identify, diagnose and manage problems, we think it important that there are systems for reporting and recording problems, and for prioritizing their investigation, and this is discussed further in later chapters.

HAS THIS PROBLEM BEEN SEEN BEFORE? CAN RECORDS ASSIST?

A patient's age and their medical history can help a medical doctor to make a successful diagnosis and plan effective treatment. Much can be learned from analogous information in organizations. But changes over time can mean that there may be important differences between the factors that caused the previous problems and those which are causing the current problems.

CAN THE PROBLEM BE ACCOMMODATED OR ITS IMPACT MITIGATED?

Suppose that targets have been missed because of the failure to recruit sufficient qualified staff. If additional qualified staff are needed for the foreseeable future, then the problem needs to be addressed. But if work is seasonal and starting to decline, or if new machinery is about to be installed and fewer staff will be required, then recruiting new staff on a permanent basis may not be the best way forward.

Achieving some 'quick fixes' may boost morale, and help meet production and other targets that are being missed. However, without some understanding of what is going on, attempting a 'quick win' could actually make things worse. For example, the common complaint that 'communications are poor' might lead to the knee-jerk reaction that all supervisors should regularly brief their staff. But, if relationships between the supervisors and the shop floor are at breaking point and the cause of the poor communications, the proposed remedial action might do more harm than good.

WHICH ORGANIZATIONAL SYSTEMS ARE INVOLVED? WHAT INFORMATION CAN THEY YIELD?

Consider a hypothetical problem of high labour turnover. In such a case, priority might be given to the systems listed in the right-hand column of Figure 5.2,

'A framework for organizational diagnosis', including personnel selection procedures and occupational training. In particular, when did labour turnover start to get worse, and were there any changes in the recruits (e.g. their age, gender or educational level) or in the work to which they were then allocated and inducted? Sources of information would include the personnel and line managers and personnel records. A quick check might also be made as to whether labour turnover has been consistent throughout the organization as a whole, or whether it has been much higher in some areas than in others? And if there have been differences between areas, departments or divisions, why might this be, are there differences in the work, the working conditions, the rates of pay, the managers, etc.

Other existing records which might yield helpful information include records of annual appraisals and of 'exit interviews'. Further, some organizations use psychometrics as part of initial selection and in subsequent assessment and development processes and analyses of trends may prove helpful – in one organization an analysis of test scores showed that the abilities of those appointed to management posts had been declining over the years in spite of the intellectual demands on managers becoming more complex. However, care may need to be taken over the release of information from personnel and other records, and anonymous summaries may need to be prepared.

Also potentially relevant are the views of employees (both informal and/or collected by means of some kind of survey), the observations of people experienced in assessing work and working conditions, and actual measurements of the work and working conditions including temperature, lighting and noise.

It is unlikely that a clear change at a precise point in time will be found. For example, the arrival of an unsatisfactory manager may not have an immediate effect – it may take a series of incidents before loyal staff decide to leave and even more time before they find alternative employment, hand in their notice and subsequently leave. Similarly it may be some time before it is clear that a changed selection procedure is producing a lower proportion of acceptable recruits.

A final consideration is whether the problems might be originating from a single or common source, such as one of the eight groups of managers described in Chapter 3.

SHOULD PEOPLE BE TOLD WHERE THEY STAND?

Most medical doctors take the view that patients should know where they stand. Even when there are signs of serious or even terminal illness, they normally give their patients the opportunity to understand their condition, so that they can come to terms with the implications and continue to manage their lives.

To conclude that an organization may not survive because of the behaviours of the management, the workforce, or even individuals might be rare. But it is not impossible if, for example, there has been miss-selling to clients, breaches of laws or regulations, or if 'rogue traders' have grossly exceeded their financial limits.

Certainly an organization's future may be in doubt if financial criteria are taken into account as well as behavioural criteria and in such circumstances it is arguably even more important that those in the organization know where they stand. This may increase their commitment to taking part in the preliminary work and to finding a way forward.

Such involvement can generate new possibilities for moving forward. Financial difficulties meant that a major football club was on the verge of closure. When the players were put in the picture, they agreed to a 75 per cent reduction in salaries, the sole condition being that none of the staff should be made redundant. Sadly this was not sufficient to ensure the future of all those in the club.

HOW ELSE CAN RAPPORT AND ENGAGEMENT BE ENCOURAGED?

Collecting information about the attitudes and views of staff at the heart of a problem can be a key part of the information required for diagnosis. Although the views of those who remain may differ from those who have recently left, it is important to know whether remaining staff are on the verge of leaving, and why? However, experienced interviewers will know that some people simply echo the views of others and that the origins of some complaints are long forgotten. Interviewers need to have the skills to 'dig deeper' with questions like 'Why do you say that?', 'How did things come to be like this?' and 'What can be done to improve things?' Just as importantly they need to know when to 'back off' or to leave a question unasked.

Credible assurances of confidentiality can increase both the numbers participating and their 'openness' about their views. Without such assurances, employees may feel that they are admitting inadequacies or even jeopardizing their future employment. At the start of one survey interview, a nervous middle-aged man sought further assurances about confidentiality. Once given, he visibly relaxed and explained that it had taken him weeks of walking the streets and knocking on doors to get his job in an area of high unemployment. Satisfied that confidence would be respected, he then rolled back his sleeves to reveal deep burns on his forearms; these had been caused by contact with hot metal tubes while putting slings around them so that they could be moved by a crane. That the tubes were still hot was not apparent to the eye, and the protective clothing provided was not adequate.

Assurances of confidentiality may help reveal some unpalatable truths – the possible root cause of an organization's malfunction can arise from any level of management, including the very top. The practical implication of this is that any individual or team should have the authority to look beyond the 'presenting problem' to satisfy them that what needs to be investigated and managed is not higher up the organization.

When assurances of confidentiality have been given, the presentation of findings must not permit the identification of individuals. This can require some skill if departments are small and individuals specialize in the work that they do. But failure to do so can put working relationships at risk and jeopardize future surveys. Following one survey, there was alarm when a personnel manager said that it had been possible to identify two individuals because of their other questionnaire responses, and that 'a word will be had with them'.

Focus groups can be used as an alternative to attitude surveys or in addition to them. While some may be reluctant to express their views in front of colleagues, hearing others express their views can encourage others to contribute.

WHEN TO STOP? CAN A 'DIAGNOSIS' BE MADE AND TREATMENT PLANNED?

Sometimes medical doctors can recognize a cluster of symptoms as being typical of a disease or other condition described by others, they can also draw on the experience of others to consider options for the management of the condition and even its successful treatment. In contrast, those working in organizations cannot yet draw on a body of information to consider the options for 'diagnosis', 'management' or 'treatment'. Accordingly, checks need to be made that emerging views about diagnosis and treatment are consistent with all the available evidence about when the problem started, when it got worse, etc.

Simple correlations are not explanations (a point once illustrated by the statement that '95 per cent of juvenile delinquents eat tomatoes'). However, correlations can provide the first clues as to what is going on, as when Dr John Snow noted that outbreaks of cholera were restricted to small part of London and traced the source to a water pump in Broad Street, Soho that was contaminated by sewage. Realization that cholera was water-borne, rather than air-borne, was a significant development in its eradication.

It is unlikely that a 'silver bullet' or other instant cure will be found, although the replacement of an ill-tempered or bullying manager may come close! Findings are more likely to suggest multiple causes and multiple effects. So the way forward may be to take a series of actions which together will reduce or even eliminate the problems being experienced.

Indeed we acknowledge that some problems can be easy to diagnose but very difficult to resolve. In one large organization the pay rates were too low to attract and retain staff in a highly specialized function. By persuading those running the organization's job evaluation scheme that prior experience was essential, the pay rates were increased and staff turnover dropped. However, the numbers of applicants with the required experience then fell too. Those running the job evaluation scheme would not allow salaries to reflect 'market rates' and the deadlock continued for years.

The main reason for seeking further information is that the information collected thus far fails to provide a coherent or convincing explanation of the causes of the problem, or generate sufficient actionable changes. It is possible too that other matters may have emerged which require investigation. If this happens, a view needs to be taken as to what additional information should be sought and who should collect it? Related questions are 'How much will this cost?', 'How will this be funded?' and 'What benefits might be anticipated?'.

In general we would caution about the possibility of 'analysis paralysis' and of the dangers of collecting even more information without having good reasons for doing so.

Once the additional information has been collected, it might be summarized by answering the following questions:

1. What now seems to be the problem?

2. What do we now see as the impact of this problem?

3. Can the problem be accommodated or its impact mitigated?

4. If action is still required, what is now known about the problem?

5. Is there now enough information to make at least a provisional diagnosis and to suggest management or even 'treatment'? Alternatively, should even more information be sought? (If so, who should collect it? How much will this cost, how will it be funded and what might the benefits be?)

6. How quickly was this problem recognized and addressed? If the delay was excessive, what needs to be done to improve the organization's 'response time' in the future?

7. Was this problem a 'one-off' or is there any evidence that this is just one of a series of problems? If there is evidence of a series of problems, might there be common causes?

8. Are 'key' staff adequate?

Planning

Managers and others want to know how long an investigation will take, and how it can be staffed and funded. Because findings cannot be predicted it is impossible to give precise answers, but key issues relevant to making a rapid initial assessment are now discussed.

THE NUMBERS INVOLVED AND HOW INFORMATION WILL BE COLLECTED

Clearly the numbers and locations of employees whose performance or behaviour is giving cause for concern will affect the time needed. However, the time required will also depend on how information is to be collected – possible methods include face-to-face or telephone interviews, on-line and other questionnaires and focus groups. All methods can indicate areas of engagement or dissatisfaction, but they vary in the extent to which they give insight as to why views are held. Questionnaire surveys may need to be followed by interviews or group discussions to find out more about the reasons for the replies.

Sampling should be considered. Where large numbers of people are doing similar work, a carefully drawn 10 per cent sample of employees (taking into account type of work done, age, gender, ethnicity, length of service, etc) may be sufficient to reflect the views of employees as a whole.

It may also be appropriate to review information about employees. This might include summary information and statistics such as labour turnover and length of service, and information from personnel records such as annual appraisals.

HOW INFORMATION WILL BE COLLATED, ANALYSED AND REPORTED

From the point of view of diagnosis, the systematic reporting of all the information collected is desirable, even though some of it may offend senior staff whose actions or policies are being criticized. It can be helpful to know both widely-held views and the sometimes insightful comments of a few. Analyses showing whether and how information varies with type of work done, age, etc may be helpful too.

DIAGNOSIS, TREATMENT, ETC.

From the point of view of planning, the subsequent stages of diagnosis, management, treatment and evaluation also need to be considered. Those who have collected, analysed and reported information from and about employees may venture views about the underlying reasons for the problems and how they might be managed or even 'treated'. The views of experts may be sought too. But in many organizations, senior or even top management will want to be involved in the diagnostic phase where there is likely to be discussion about the information collected, the underlying reasons, and what to do next. Indeed, really complex problems might best involve a group of senior and experienced managers such as a sub-committee of the board of directors/governors, Council of Management or whatever the ruling body is. Senior people may also want to be involved because of the cost and other implications of remedial and other actions.

MANAGEMENT, TREATMENT AND EVALUATION

Resulting action can range from the replacement of a supervisor in a small department to a review of policies that could ultimately have ramifications for the whole of a multinational organization. Resulting training and other initiatives may last for years or even become a permanent feature.

Provision should also be made for evaluation. This should not only include an assessment of whether the problems were resolved without new problems emerging, but also evaluations of the cost-effectiveness of the investigation and of the performance of the staff involved.

COULD A PRELIMINARY INVESTIGATION BE HELPFUL?

Some years ago, it was common for organization-wide attitude surveys to be carried out in order to find out more about specific issues. However, the issues were sometimes confined to particular departments and it became clear that shorter investigations that focussed only on these areas would be more effective and more efficient. Indeed, medical doctors do not arrange comprehensive investigations of all an individual's body systems when a patient appears to have a minor problem with just one of them.

So it may be possible to identify and 'target' specific problems (such as the recruitment of teachers described earlier) rather than review the whole of an organization's selection and training processes. Alternatively, it may be possible to investigate those work groups where turnover is high rather than cover a whole organization. Enough information may emerge for a comprehensive investigation to be unnecessary.

A preliminary investigation can also assist the planning of a much larger investigation. For example, if a major multinational company is concerned about high wastage among its graduate trainees, the numbers of graduates and the variety of their work and work locations may mean that a 'pilot study' could help determine how a more detailed investigation might be carried out.

HOW MIGHT AN INVESTIGATION BE STAFFED?

So that an organization can better learn when and how to do investigations of this kind we suggest that a senior manager or committee of managers should be responsible for their management and evaluation.

The *information collection phase* is likely to need staff with some expertise in interviewing and other survey methods, and in building a data base. Staff collecting information from employees should respect confidentiality and be independent too. For example, personnel staff may claim that a supervisor's behaviour is causing staff to leave, while production staff may claim that the people recruited by personnel staff have been unsuitable. To ask a member of staff directly involved in the dispute to investigate it further, be it from the personnel or the production functions, would lead to suspicions that the investigation and subsequent recommendations would be biased.

Large organizations may have individuals based elsewhere who would be seen as independent – they might include people working in a different division or in the organization's headquarters; this could be an excellent development for potential top managers. Other options might include post-graduate students seeking projects as part of their higher degree course and external consultants.

For projects needing more than one person, a special team might be formed comprising a mixture of internal staff, contract staff, etc. Survey and other skills likely to be required have already been described. In addition, if the work group being investigated does work that is complex or demands specialist knowledge, a person with the relevant technical background might be sought to join the investigating team. Ideally there might be a balance between staff who place great store on the systematic collection and analyses of facts, and those who are more intuitive in their approach and sensitive to the possibility of difficulties being the result, for example, of apparent bias, prejudice or simple misunderstanding.

However, there needs to be clarity about the scope of the team's activities, particularly the extent to which they will be involved in the subsequent diagnostic and other phases. Ideally team members should have the opportunity to appreciate each others' skills and expertise before the investigation starts. The stages in building an effective group have been described as 'forming', 'storming', 'norming ' and 'performing'. 'Mock' scenarios might be discussed and feedback given from an experienced chairman or facilitator. Members might also be trained in one of the approaches to root-cause analysis set out at the beginning of the next chapter. For example, the National Health Institute for Innovation and Improvement provides training in '5 Whys' questioning on demand for National Health Service (NHS) Trusts.

The formation of a special team could be an attractive proposition for a large organization if there may be several such issues to be investigated. However, this is unlikely to be cost-effective for a one-off project and small organizations may decide to seek external assistance.

Staffing the diagnostic phase may be complicated by the wish of an organization's top management to be involved. This may be a 'mixed blessing'. On the one hand the top staff may have additional relevant background information, and may also be able to see how possible remedial action might complement or conflict with other policies and procedures. On the other hand they may lack diagnostic skills. Further, the information collected may be raising questions or concerns about areas for which they are responsible, and power and prejudice may be evoked. If survey data indicates that it is the behaviour of the chairman or CEO that is causing an organization's sickness, how can an effective meeting be planned and held?

Indeed, any formal meetings may only be a part of what happens. Prior to the meeting there may be extensive discussions as options are evaluated, and at the formal meeting directors may be simply asked to choose between options or to approve a single recommendation.

Large organizations may want to identify top or senior managers to specialize in diagnostic work and develop their skills. Again small organizations may decide to seek external assistance, perhaps asking a consultant to train their top management in diagnostic skills or even attend diagnostic meetings as an advisor.

Staffing implications of the management and treatment phase are impossible to predict. However, it is possible that some 'treatments' can be deployed by existing staff after appropriate training.

If all these issues are taken into account, staffing decisions can require some shrewd judgements. In particular, if it is suspected that the policies or behaviours of senior or even top managers are causing the problems, the investigation must be led by people who can deal with their defensiveness and help the organization to move forward.

HOW MIGHT AN INVESTIGATION BE FUNDED?

Even in a small investigation involving a single department, some costs will be incurred. It is normal for staff to take part in surveys in work time. And there is the cost of analysis and the search for patterns or trends that could inform diagnosis. There is also the time required to discuss the findings and agree, implement and monitor appropriate action.

However, this has to be balanced against any costs or loss of business incurred by failing to meet targets. Further, if problems can be resolved and Organizational Fitness improved, there may be ultimate gains in terms of lower employee turnover rates, improved attendance and timekeeping, improved product quality, suggestions for better ways of working and improved products, etc.

Concluding Comments

We have aimed to identify and discuss the features of good preparation for diagnosis – the organizational equivalent of a doctor examining a patient and taking a case-history. Planning should anticipate a multi-stage iterative process which involves collecting and analysing information until explanations of what has happened can be reached, diagnosis confirmed and management can be planned on a rational basis. That said, a preliminary study, or a pause after the initial collection of data, might yield sufficient information for diagnosis, management and even treatment to start.

Ultimately, the desirability of systematically developing a logical explanation and a soundly-based action plan needs to be weighed against the need to sustain production, motivate staff and keep the organization alive. Although there are dangers in seeking 'quick fixes' it would be wrong to delay taking 'reasonable' action if an organization's survival is threatened.

Organizations may wish to develop expertise in these kinds of investigations by asking a senior person to manage and evaluate them, and we have discussed planning in general and staffing in particular. There is also the question of whether an individual or group should specialize in diagnostic work; they might also be involved in the processes involved in moving Towards Organizational Fitness which can require many common skills. These issues are discussed further in Chapters 7 and 9.

Chapter 5

Diagnosis

This chapter will briefly review the history of organizational diagnosis, give some illustrative scenarios of the issues involved and what can be learned from them, ask whether current approaches to diagnosis are 'fit for purpose', introduce a 'systems approach to organizational diagnosis' and discuss how the approach might be used in practice before making some brief concluding comments.

But first, some thoughts about how much time and effort should be devoted to diagnosis. In the previous chapter we acknowledged that there may not be time for thorough and systematic preparation. A similar comment must be made here. Detailed discussions with medical doctors suggest that, in initial consultations, general practitioners have two issues at the front of their minds. One is whether and how the symptoms might be managed and perhaps treated. The other is whether the symptoms could be the first signs of a potentially serious or even fatal condition.

So if organizational symptoms suggest a potentially serious or fatal condition, moving quickly to managing symptoms could be justified. In such circumstances we would suggest that some of the organization's best brains should be quickly summoned to form an overview of what is going on and to develop plans for managing the situation; this might include any staff who are specializing in diagnosis or improving fitness. Care must be taken that action aimed at resolving one problem does not have an adverse impact on another.

However, we also warn that some may exaggerate the severity of problems in order to justify quick 'knee-jerk' and possibly inappropriate action being taken and we would again emphasise the need for a more systematic investigation once the crisis has passed.

In contrast, just as doctors may help patients to manage their symptoms without coming to a firm view about diagnosis, so those doing diagnostic work in organizations are likely to be judged on the effectiveness of their recommendations for managing the problems. For both, there will be criticism of excessive thoroughness and unnecessary investigations.

The History of Organizational Diagnosis

In the pre-history of management, diagnosis would appear to be based on belief, opinion, then intuition. Over time there came the use of 'check lists'. It would be interesting to know when people started to make a list of things to do before they commenced a journey or task, probably a very long time ago, and then learned to double back through the checklist when something goes wrong. Then along came what can be called 'systematic intuition', now the trend is towards sophisticated multivariate statistical analysis. The first efforts towards systematic intuition appeared in the middle of the last century. The most practical and influential was developed within the Japanese car manufacturer Toyota, called the '5 Whys' technique. The ideas behind it can be traced back to the founder, Sakichi Toyoda, of the company that originally manufactured textile machinery in the nineteenth century. Essentially it involved a series, of usually five, penetrating questions about a problem that was causing difficulties. This questioning approach was enhanced in the 1960s by Ishikawa who developed it into a 'Fishbone Diagram', then further developed into a 'Fault Tree Analysis'.

A more theoretical parallel line of techniques can be seen to have started in the 1950s with Kurt Lewin's 'Force Field Analysis', which was first enhanced by Leavitt's, then Likert's, 'System Analysis'. Once systems thinking burst on the scene a plethora of models followed, such as Weisbord's 'Six-box Model', Kepner-Tregoe's 'Rational Manager', McKinsey's '7S Framework', Tichy's 'Technical Political Cultural Framework', the Nadler-Tushman 'Congruence Model', the Nelson-Burns' 'High-Performance Programming', Harrison's 'Model for Diagnosing Individual and Group Behaviour', the Burke-Litwin 'Model of Organizational Performance and Change', the Sociotechnical Systems Approach originating from the Tavistock Institute and more recently Falletta's 'Organizational Intelligence Model'.

This brief review shows that there is not yet a generally agreed model for organizational diagnosis. What the above approaches have in common is the essential use of skilled, directed interviewing to collect information systematically, the need to take into account a large range of variables that can influence the performance of an organization and finally an attempt to focus on an outcome, the 'Root Cause' of the problem. The trend within them is towards greater complexity of statistical analysis and the use of computers to analyse the data. In contrast, what practicing, thoughtful managers require for everyday use are more simple models that help to direct information gathering and analysis more directly to the root causes of organizational malfunctioning. An attempt to provide this is given later in the chapter.

In medicine, diagnosis is the determination of the causes of diseases by the symptoms. For medical doctors the good news is that others may have documented a description of the combination of symptoms associated with a disease together with information about the effectiveness of their attempts at treatment. The bad news is that some almost identical combination of symptoms can have very different underlying causes and this means a treatment that is effective for one possible underlying condition could be fatal if the same symptoms are caused by one of the alternative underlying diseases. Much was made of the pressures and dilemmas facing doctors attempting to diagnose and treat gravely ill patients in the popular television series 'House'.

According to Wikipedia, *diagnosis* (from an ancient Greek word for discernment) is 'the identification of the nature and cause of a certain phenomenon'. Diagnosis is used in many different disciplines with variations in the use of logics, analytics, and experience to determine *cause and effect*. In systems engineering and computer science, it is typically used to determine the causes of symptoms, mitigations, and solutions.

In practice, diagnosis is likely to be one part of an iterative cycle involving four activities:

a)   Preparation and examination (Chapter 4).

b)   Diagnosis (this chapter).

c)   Management – which may include the trial of possible treatments.

d)   Monitoring (Chapter 6).

These phases can overlap and the time and resources required for the phases may change as the study progresses.

Scenarios to Illustrate Organizational Diagnoses

The following scenarios provide examples of how some basic organizational diagnoses have been carried out. All involved an external consultant well aware of the wide range of potential causes of organizational problems and familiar with some of the approaches to organizational diagnosis described earlier. However, fees (and hence time) had to be agreed ahead of the work being done when it was impossible to know what findings would emerge.

It can be seen that the recommendations made were based directly on the results of the investigation. These scenarios contrast with the case studies presented at the start of the next chapter where the recommendations proposed went well beyond the views expressed by staff who were interviewed during attitude surveys.

SCENARIO 1: HIGH LABOUR TURNOVER AMONG PHARMACEUTICAL MANUFACTURING STAFF

This scenario concerned the investigation of high labour turnover among staff in a pharmaceutical manufacturing company. Individual interviews were held with a sample of existing employees and assurances of confidentiality were given.

For a number of reasons, staff interviewed were not overly enthusiastic about their work. In particular, some commented on the need to wear masks and said that when they started work the atmosphere had seemed to be unfriendly. Because of the masks it was difficult to hear what was said and some commented that it was only when they started to look at the eyes of their colleagues that they realized that people were friendly and smiling, something that they had missed when first working with people whose mouths (and noses) were covered by the masks.

The written report to management addressed the wide range of issues reported, but paid particular attention to the need to help new employees to communicate with their colleagues in spite of the restrictions arising from the face masks.

Comments About Scenario 1

Questions might have been asked as to whether turnover rates had varied over time (and why) and why the organization's own staff had not tried to investigate the problem. That said, the fact that the investigation was carried out by an independent person and assurances of confidentiality were given might again have helped make staff feel that they could describe their experiences and express their feelings. More effort might have been made to find out whether the recommended action was effective.

SCENARIO 2: HIGH LABOUR TURNOVER AMONG STAFF IN A PLASTICS FACTORY

Asked to investigate high labour turnover in a manufacturing company because production targets were not being met, it was proposed that a first step should be to identify where the turnover was occurring. Analysis showed that the highest turnover of over 300 per cent per annum was on the night shift of one department and subsequent investigations focused on this shift. Local management had not been aware of this. The working conditions in the department were extremely noisy and staff found it difficult to communicate with each other. Pay was said to be poor when compared with other departments and with other employers in the area. During the hours that the investigators were there, the supervisor remained in his office apparently reading magazines with a content that many would find offensive.

This was the UK site of an overseas-owned company and senior overseas-based managers were attempting to run the company by making regular visits and by having production and other reports sent to them on an almost daily basis. This meant that the UK managers spent their time collecting information and sending it overseas and had very little discretion to investigate and improve things themselves.

In the written report to management it was recommended that the UK managers should have more scope to investigate problems and improve things as appropriate. This could include attempts at noise reduction in the department where turnover had been highest. That said, there were obvious reasons to be concerned about the performance of the supervisor and this raised questions about his selection, training and subsequent management.

Comments About Scenario 2

The organization's overseas management had recognized that overall turnover was unacceptably high, but they had no time to investigate where it was occurring or the reasons for it during their brief visits. Nor had they asked local management to investigate it. With hindsight, more questions might have been asked about the appropriateness of this way of managing.

SCENARIO 3: HIGH LABOUR TURNOVER IN ENGINEERING COMPANY

At the start of the study, managers said that hourly-paid employees wanted to get out of engineering because of a spate of local redundancies in the industry. But an investigation of factory personnel records at the start of the study showed turnover to be far higher in some departments than in others. During interviews with those working in departments with high turnover, many expressed particular concern about pay. They said that as a result of a recent job evaluation, their work was now paid at the lowest rates in the factory and there were no opportunities for overtime. They also said that others had been leaving for more money elsewhere and asked how we would manage on the money that they were being paid. None of them expressed any fears of redundancy.

The written report submitted to management drew attention to the apparently close relationship between labour turnover and pay rates and recommended that the latter should be reviewed.

Comments About Scenario 3

The organization's own staff had recognized that turnover was unacceptably high. But instead of trying to pinpoint the areas in which turnover was highest they had attributed it to a wish to 'get out of engineering'. It was not clear how that view had been formed. Further, those who were interviewed showed no hesitation in expressing their views as to what was wrong. Obviously, if a diagnosis is wrong, the treatment will be ineffective if not harmful. This is something to bear in mind in situations where treatments have been tried but have proved ineffective or have even made matters worse.

The Scenarios and Diagnosis

In our view the above scenarios raise five issues worthy of discussion.

LOCAL DIAGNOSES MAY NOT HAVE BEEN ATTEMPTED NOR BE CORRECT

Experience has taught the cynical television character Dr House that nobody tells the (whole) truth and while we do not endorse his manner we share his view that the accuracy and completeness of local information and the related diagnoses may be suspect. Indeed, it is sometimes because the efforts of local management to diagnose and treat problems have been unsuccessful that consultants and others become involved. We don't know of any studies which indicate the proportion of problems which are solved by local management. But clearly some local diagnoses may not be correct and any which propose expensive remedial action should be scrutinized.

THOSE WHO COLLECT DIAGNOSTIC INFORMATION DO NOT NEED TO HAVE EXPERTISE IN |DIAGNOSIS

In the world of medicine, a wide array of technical staff make assessments on behalf of doctors, providing test results and other information which doctors can take into account when diagnosing sickness. Although some technical staff can be very highly qualified and their experience may be invaluable in the diagnostic process, ultimate responsibility lies with the medical doctor in charge of the patient. We see parallels in organizational work. People who can analyse personnel records or carry out attitude surveys can contribute greatly to the diagnostic process, but it would be wrong to assume that they should have responsibility either for the actual diagnosis or the subsequent treatment. The issue of who is to be responsible for investigation as a whole and the diagnostic element within it must be addressed.

SOME PROBLEMS CAN BE TRACED TO SPECIFIC LOCATIONS OR GROUPS

The scenarios described earlier in this chapter illustrate how problems such as labour turnover can sometimes be traced to particular departments. In certain circumstances it could also be appropriate to carry out analysis by age, length of service, gender, ethnic origin, management grade, etc.

LINKING SYMPTOMS AND THEIR CAUSES

The figures provided earlier in this book about how organizations work may help those attempting diagnosis to see possible connections. Note that the figures show activities rather than job titles and in some organizations it may take some time to find whether the activity exists, who is responsible for it and the views of those responsible for its effectiveness. Indeed, one potential reason for problems may be that nobody has been allocated responsibility for the activity. Some years ago this was the case in one large organization which provided local delivery staff with bicycles, nobody was responsible for training staff in the maintenance of the bicycles.

MAKING MORE USE OF HISTORICAL INFORMATION

Medical doctors find that diagnosis is greatly assisted by medical records since many medical conditions are associated with a patient's age and medical history. Further, medical records can indicate whether a treatment has worked or whether a patient has had allergic or other reactions.

Interestingly it seems to be rare for those doing diagnostic work to be given the results of previous investigations of the same or similar problems. This may be because of the turnover of management staff – in many organizations, managers, particularly successful managers who are considered to have potential, are moved on after three years or so to broaden their experience. This may mean that reports exist but have been forgotten and it may be worth making enquiries to see if any can be traced.

Are Current Approaches to Diagnosis 'Fit for Purpose?'

Thus far in this chapter we have concentrated on what can be done given the current states of knowledge and practice. However, it is one of the main points of this book is that there will be times when more effort will need to be put into diagnosing *exactly* what is wrong with an organization before considering how to manage any emerging problems and perhaps implement a treatment and the above scenarios tend to support that view.

Why is this? The first possible explanation is the difficulty of carrying out diagnoses. The history of medicine reveals that in early times there were just a few treatments that were applied to any malady. The practice was to search for a universal cure for all ills. For example, blood letting, often using leeches, was a general cure-all, comparable today to 'down-sizing' or 'out-placing' by organizations! Perhaps one of the strengths of early Chinese medicine was the greater effort put into diagnosis, this being probably triggered by the wide range of herbal remedies available. Having so many cures forces a 'doctor' to be much more precise about the prescribed treatment. Consequently the key to any therapy is an exact diagnosis. Only too often people are treated for illnesses they do not have, or do not get treatment for the real cause of their pain or suffering. So too, with organizations where there are also many therapies used which do not match the cause of the symptoms. The consequent waste and unnecessary suffering arising from not treating the real cause of the sickness must be rampant in organizations throughout the world.

Why are diagnostic investigations so few and shallow in comparison to the plethora of organizational treatments? It could be that certain members of an organization do not want a true diagnosis in case it reflects unfavourably on them and requires them to change. For all manner of reasons, such as they do not want:

- to be blamed;

- to change;

- to own up;

- to feel responsible;

- to lose face; or

- feel inadequate, to know they are a part of a failing organization.

So they resist a thorough diagnostic investigation, the more they feel responsible the stronger they are likely to resist. Perhaps this may be a useful indicator of where to start to look for the source of an organization's sickness!

Severely ill people are obvious both to themselves and to other people. So too with organizations. A really sick organization is obvious to all its staff and to observant visitors and customers, with perhaps a few right at the top of it who are out of touch, have their heads in the sand and are oblivious to the realities of their situation. It is the large number of unwell people and organizations who are in the middle range of health that are difficult to diagnose. Often they do not want to know that they are ill and then to face up to all the consequences and practical implications of finding out.

The signs and signals that are listed in Appendix A are useful indicators that something is wrong but they do not provide much help in deciding the root causes of the malaise. What is required is a more systematic approach to collecting the 'symptoms' so that the real causes of the sickness are identified. This is where so called 'systems approaches to organizational development' can be useful as the following models display.

Systems Approaches to Organizational Diagnosis

The first issue is the size of the problem. Is the organizational malfunction not due to anything within the organization but within the world of work itself? These are the big questions of political and religious philosophy, sociology, culture and economic climate. Such possibilities for the source of the sicknesses of work organizations require a macro-approach to diagnosis. An attempt to do this is set out in Figure 5.1 below.

Figure 5.1 is developed from Figure 3.1 in Chapter 3. Such a model is probably of more use to politicians and academics than practicing managers, who experience the effects of these macro-issues but are usually powerless,

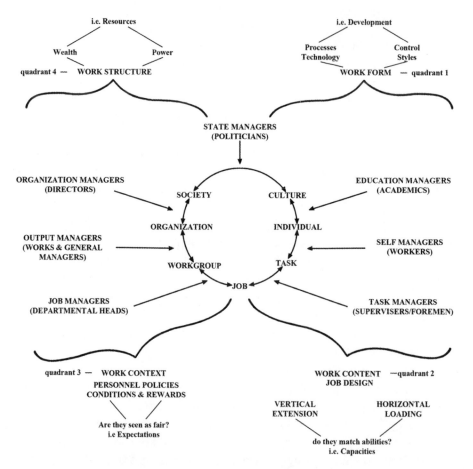

Figure 5.1   **A closed system of the main interactions and problems between individuals, managers and society**

beyond making representations through their professional and trade associations to government departments, to do anything about them. However, a detailed analysis of the quadrants displays possible conflicts and problems that organization managers have to handle and if they get these wrong then some kind of sickness will result.

Quadrant 1 concerns the form that work can take, the processes and technology that are available and how the work is controlled. None of these processes are static, some develop at a considerable pace, such as the application of computers. Consequently they can either enhance the productivity of an organization or run it into the ground. So too with the developments in control styles. The trend here has been a progressive movement away from authoritarian management styles towards more democratic and participative styles. However some managers cannot cope with the new relationships required and the skills to handle them while some workers cannot cope with the new responsibilities given to them.

Quadrant 2 concerns the content of the work, how jobs are designed and how the tasks within them are grouped. The conflict here is between workers being given more of the same to carry out or having their job 'enriched' with other interesting tasks and responsibilities. The issue of 'individual differences' arises. While, some people enjoy the routine of a production line or call-centre, others are bored out of their minds. How to handle this is put forward later in the chapter with Figure 5.3.

Quadrant 3 concerns the context within which work is performed. The personnel policies that they are subsumed under and the working conditions and rewards that are provided for carrying them out. The key issues here are fairness and expectations. Who gets what of the 'organizational cake' and how it is justified can provide great bones of contention, even to grind an organization to a halt.

Finally, Quadrant 4 is concerned with the structure of the organization, particularly the supply of resources and power through ownership. The issue here is who owns what? This quadrant can be a great source of conflict within an organization.

In each of these quadrants are sources of problems and difficulties that confront all work organizations. Unless all the 'managers' of the key interactions are doing a good job the organization will malfunction. So in any diagnostic process their effectiveness should be questioned.

The next level of diagnosis is at the level of the work organization itself. This is where an open systems approach is particularly useful. It is here that the society/culture in which the organization exists provides the input for the organization and makes use of the goods and services that the organization creates. A diagrammatic description of an open system that can be used to describe and explain the process of transforming worker behaviour into valued commodities is set out in Figure 5.2 below. This model is a derivative of Figure 3.2, used in Chapter 3 to illustrate how organizations work, as such it is of greater relevance than the model in Figure 3.2 to providing a basis for the diagnosis of organizational malfunctioning. The rather simple and static form of the model in Figure 3.2 is developed into a more dynamic model that focuses on the interactions between the components.

Figure 5.2 provides the opportunity for taking a step-by-step approach to questioning each of the main components that determine how well an organization works. The individual/group carrying out the diagnosis will

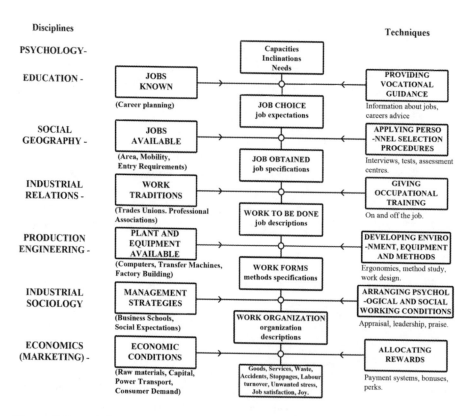

Figure 5.2   A framework for organizational diagnosis

then discover whether there is sufficient information available under the headings to judge how well that component functions. If not, a data gathering exercise should then take place. All this is comparable to a medical practitioner questioning patients about their symptoms, forming a view about which physiological systems (such as the respiratory system) may not be functioning correctly and then deciding whether further tests, such as scans and X-rays, are required to effect an exact diagnosis. The advocacy of a systematic approach

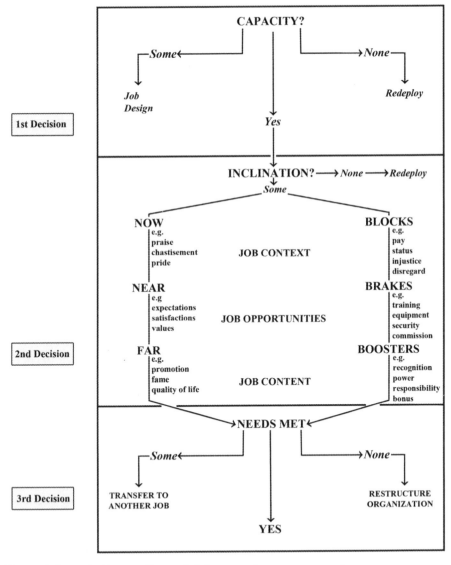

Figure 5.3   A diagnostic model for people management

to organizational diagnosis is a cornerstone of this book and what is suggested above is just a start.

Organizational sickness can be due to the sum total of all the individual workers' work-related inadequacies or even just the inefficiency, ineptness, or bitterness of one or a few key members of staff, using the term to include all the members of the organization! This can be analysed by a further model, as set out in Figure 5.3.

This model indicates that three crucial decisions have to be made about the work and well-being of an individual worker. This model can be used when a manager sits down with a member of staff to discuss how the individual is getting on in their job. It can also be used as the structure for a performance review or appraisal interview, or indeed the foundation of a performance management programme. The first question to consider is has s/he the capacity required for the job? If the answer is 'no', then the individual should be helped to choose another job. If the answer is just 'some', then job re-design or further training will be needed to be considered to make the job within the range of capacities that the individual possesses, if such a person-centred personnel policy exists within the organization! If the answer is 'yes' discussion should focus on what the individual, manager or organization should be doing differently *next* that would add to that capacity, i.e. an action plan.

Once that has been achieved, and hopefully committed to by all involved, the manager should proceed to discuss the level of motivation the individual has for the job and what can be done to increase it. When asked, it appears that the job is not to the individual's liking and their inclination to carry on with it is low, then they would need to be deployed elsewhere, perhaps even outside the organization. If the individual has some inclination for the job then what can be done to add to that inclination needs to be explored. The bi-furcated section in the centre of this model embraces the whole area of motivational theory, another book in itself! Suffice to say that as everyone's needs are different to add to an individual's level of motivation their next need should be identified and action taken to meet it, or at least go towards meeting it. Giving someone something they do not need nor want does nothing to their motivation, nor the extent to which they 'feel good' about the organization. Failing to identify and provide what an individual is really hoping for can bring about frustration and even alienation. The central section of this model classifies all the sources of motivation set out in text books on the subject, the categories on the left are behavioural and on the right are structural. The model illustrates the fundamental issue in psychology of 'individual differences', everyone's capacities, inclinations and needs are different so each individual needs to be managed differently and this model shows how a manager can go about doing this. If such a process is carried out for each and every individual making up the organization and decisions made and action plans put in place to apply them for each and every member of staff then the whole organization would not fail to become more effective and a happier place to work in. Sadly there are employees, at all levels, where the rather person-centred approach set out in Figure 5.3 just does not work despite the exercise of considerable inter-personal skill. In such cases more drastic action will need to be taken, and this is set out in Appendix B, 'When individuals threaten the future of an organization'.

It could be that if managers regularly interact with their staff, using the above model, many of the behavioural issues that beset organizations would not arise in the first place, so reducing the need to spend time and effort on the more formal methods of organizational diagnosis set out in this book. If applying this model does not appear to have a widespread beneficial affect, then this would point to a deeper structural issue besetting the organization, so triggering a formal process of diagnosis.

Using the Models in Practice

All these models and approaches can be used to assemble and organize information in a systematic way about what is going on both within and around the organization that is affecting its health. They can be used to train those people who make up the 'diagnostic teams', discussed in Chapter 4.

The first decision that the diagnostic team has to make is whether the malaise is primarily structural that is due to the way the organization is structured, the distribution of power and resources throughout the organization and the laid down systems and procedures that are expected to be followed, or primarily behavioural, that is the way staff are managed and how they interact with each other as individuals, teams, and departments. Once that has been done they can then move on to searching for the 'root causes'. They can do this by working systematically through the questions about all the components and interactions identified in the model, questioning what is going on and discussing how things should be different.

Concluding Comments

This chapter has discussed three things. First, scenarios have shown how problems can be diagnosed and suggestions for their management can be made. Then there has been discussion of the potential complexity and difficulty of getting to the root cause of an organization's problems. Finally, systems approaches have been proposed and described to tackle the process of organizational diagnosis. Even in potentially catastrophic circumstances there should be an attempt at systematic diagnosis before embarking on any organizational treatment! This will determine the treatment that will be required, the focus of the next chapter.

Chapter 6
Identifying and Evaluating Possible Strategies and Treatments

Having encouraged the systematic collection of information about symptoms and a logical approach to diagnosis, there is now the matter of how to determine which organizational treatment, or combination of treatments, will be most effective. Often there will be a wide range of options including some past and present 'fashionable solutions'.

'Treatments' do not need to be restricted to a single action. For example, in tackling a problem of high labour turnover, it may be decided to improve recruitment and selection, induction and job-related training, working conditions and rewards. Sometimes it will be necessary to plan the introduction of these actions in an appropriate order, for example, decisions may need to be made about the potential of individuals before there is heavy investment in training them individually or as part of a team.

Any 'treatment' likely to be deployed should be normally discussed with those that will be affected by it before plans are finalised, as reactions and comments may be helpful. Similarly, it may be helpful to pilot and review any major 'treatment' programme before it is fully deployed.

This is because there may be scope for improving 'treatments' and some may have unforeseen adverse effects. For example, when staff were being trained in how to use a new computer system, most wanted to know how to do things on the new system that they had been able to do on the old. However, the tutors that were hired to explain the new system had no knowledge of the old system and were unable to answer the questions. The programme had to be stopped for this to be remedied.

Scenario 1: Treatment(s) Directly Related to the Problems Identified

Here we consider treatment(s) directly related to the diagnostic information collected. For example, in some of the scenarios in the previous chapter, there were complaints about staff induction, the work and working conditions, and rates of pay. A 'direct response' would be to draw up action plans which address each issue in turn.

However, there needs to be caution about making an automatic 'direct response' for three reasons. First, it would be prudent to verify complaints arising from surveys to check the precise details and to make sure that they are genuine and not the result of malice or the activities of people with political or other agendas. One reported study described a situation in which the top industrial relations people of an automobile company were meeting to discuss an urgent labour problem. A confused issue about work rules had suddenly arisen in three stamping plants and there was a serious danger of a wildcat strike that would shut them all down. In turn this would stop all the assembly lines at a time when the peak sales period was approaching.

Initially, the industrial relations people focused on the plant from which demands appear to be most strident but eventually there was speculation that someone might have worked up a possible wildcat strike to get added leverage for his own position. It was then speculated that if something like that was going on a particular union official might be involved.

Enquiries revealed that the particular union official was deeply involved and that the dispute had nothing to do with work rules. With this new insight as to what the problem really was, management changed their approach and were able to resolve the situation.

A second reason for urging caution about simply making a 'direct response' is that many of the actions will have cost implications and/or demand excessive management or other resources, so they may need to be prioritized or phased in. A scoring system can be helpful to assist the evaluation of options in which the importance of each option is multiplied by its likely benefit.

Third, there is the possibility that addressing just some of the issues might have a beneficial effect. In the Hawthorne Studies in Chicago in the 1930s it was found that improvements in lighting levels led to improved production. However, in a further phase of the work, the lighting levels were decreased and it was found that production improved again. The researchers concluded that production was more dependent on the interest taken in the group rather than the level of lighting.

Further evidence of the importance of the social side of work came from another pioneering American study, this time in offal-cutting rooms. Morale dropped when staff were moved to superior new premises because work-groups were broken up and the social side of work declined.

So while we would not endorse work being done in poorly lit or even hazardous conditions and would urge compliance with legal and health and safety requirements, we would not normally recommend extreme comfort or even luxury. Few people expect their work and working conditions to be perfect and good supervisors can get the best out of people in spite of there being some marginal problems.

Scenario 2: Diagnosis That 'Remedial Action' is Required

In a second kind of scenario, expert investigation of initial complaints leads to a 'diagnosis' that remedial action is required. This is illustrated by two case studies.

CASE STUDY 1: A FAILING APPRAISAL SCHEME

An external consultant was asked to investigate an appraisal scheme which had lost credibility among the managers using it. Interviews were held both with managers who were doing the appraising and those who had been appraised.

When the scheme had been introduced, managers were told that one of the possible outcomes was to recommend attendance at external training courses. It transpired that, in the first round of appraisals following the introduction of the scheme, virtually all those appraised were recommended for places on external courses. This greatly exceeded the organization's budget for external training which was barely sufficient to cover the cost of a single training course. Because expectations had been raised and the recommended training had not materialsed, the whole scheme had fallen into disrepute.

However, this was not the only problem. It had become clear that some managers disliked doing appraisals but had not been offered any training or other support. When their staff asked when they were going to have an appraisal interview, managers reminded them of brief conversations about their performance on a part of a project and claimed that had been their appraisal interview. One manager nearing retirement had hoped to raise the issue of exactly when he would be retiring, the size of his pension and whether there might be some opportunity for consultancy work after he had retired. When he asked his manager when he was going to have an appraisal interview he was simply told that he was too old.

Those familiar with systems thinking will know that problems can arise if a number of people can access resources which appear to be free and available but which in practice are limited. On this occasion it was recommended that those responsible for doing appraisals should be brought together to discuss the design of the scheme and its objectives and limitations and should then be offered written guidance and training before a revised version of the scheme was reintroduced. The recommendations were accepted.

Case Study 1: Comments

Management had correctly concluded that the appraisal scheme needed review. The findings and recommendations were accepted and while the scheme continued a number of changes were made to make it more effective.

CASE STUDY 2: A SHORTAGE OF APPLICANTS FOR SUPERVISORY POSTS

An external consultant was asked to investigate the reasons why there was a shortage of applicants for supervisory posts within a pharmaceutical manufacturing company. Individual interviews were held with a sample of existing supervisors and charge-hands and also with a sample of shop-floor employees from which charge-hands and supervisors had been recruited in the past. Assurances of confidentiality were given.

Existing supervisors and charge-hands said that they had been encouraged to apply for promotion, but when appointed had not been given any training or support. In addition, production records and other forms had to be completed and no training had been given in doing this either. They did not feel that the additional money paid for being a charge-hand or a supervisor was sufficient compensation for the extra responsibility and for the fact that they could no longer chat with their friends while doing routine packing and other work on the production line.

Those working on the shop floor expressed very similar views. In particular, they were deterred from applying by the obvious need for form filling and record keeping and did not think that they would have the necessary skills to do it.

The written report submitted to management recommended that the pay of charge-hands and supervisors should be reviewed to make that aspect of the work more attractive. It also recommended that training and support should be provided to supervisors and charge-hands, particularly those who were newly appointed.

Case Study 2: Comments

The organization's own staff had recognized that turnover among those appointed to be a supervisor had been unacceptably high, but again there was no evidence that they had attempted to investigate the reasons. With hindsight, questions might have been asked about why this was. Again the fact that the investigation was carried out by an independent person and assurances of confidentiality were given might have been critical in making staff feel that they could describe their experiences and express their feelings.

Case Study 2: Sequel

The organization was pleased with the report. It turned out that, in its early days, the organization had taken considerable care over the selection and training of its supervisors and had achieved recognition for its work in that area. However, for reasons which were not clear, the programmes to select, train and support supervisors had been discontinued over the years.

The consultant who had carried out the diagnostic study was invited to design and implement selection procedures for charge-hands and supervisors that would be open to both internal and external staff. These were designed along assessment centre lines so that applicants had to show their potential to tackle a range of tasks typical of those done by supervisors. Particular attention was paid to the skills required to complete production records.

The company was delighted with the calibre of the new supervisors and the consultant concerned was offered work on a wide range of projects at the company over the subsequent years.

Again this scenario shows that the Organizational Treatment can go beyond simply addressing the specific points raised by employees. Of course, more radical solutions can be considered too, such as automation, computerization and even outsourcing.

Scenario 3: Dealing with Multiple Problems

Multiple problems can be identified when, for example, attitude surveys are carried out at a number of manufacturing or other sites.

Again, one approach would be to try and prioritize these problems and then deal with the most serious, but the number of problems and the cost of addressing each one in turn is likely to be prohibitive both in terms of time and cost.

A second approach involves analysing the problems to see to what extent they may be related or interconnected – in broad terms this is the application of Systems Thinking. The aim of the analysis is to try and identify initiatives which will, (a) simultaneously have a positive impact on several of the problem areas, and (b) which are likely to be adopted and deployed by local management. For example, improved selection methods can reduce the time needed for induction and other training, increase engagement and reduce labour turnover.

It is important to try and evaluate the full impact of possible solutions before they are implemented. This is illustrated by events at one large organization which was persuaded that a series of training initiatives would improve both the performance and morale of its workforce. To that end, the initiatives were signed off by the organization's board of directors and various training packs and other directions were sent to local managers who often had twenty or thirty people working for them.

What had not been taken into account was how much of the manager's time these training initiatives would take and eventually this was calculated to be more than 40 hours a week – this was in excess of the manager's weekly working hours!

In our experience, large centrally organized companies are vulnerable to these kinds of errors of judgement in which local managers and staff are bombarded by initiatives from headquarters without the resources to carry them out. How can such errors be avoided?

A while ago the headquarters of a major British retail organization was moved away from a shopping area. This drew complaints from the purchasing staff working in the headquarters who had been making regular visits to the store close to the old headquarters site in order to see how customers were reacting to the goods that they had purchased once they were on display for sale. Either there was no consultation about the move or the findings were ignored.

Another example of this kind of analysis and problem solving can involve what to do about falling sales. A knee-jerk reaction might be to cut prices or to run advertizing campaigns to try and attract new customers. But a more considered approach would be to try and unearth the reasons for the falling sales and take corrective action based on these reasons – the more effective solutions might be to improve the product specification, increase prices and focus on customer retention.

Although less rigorous in terms of data collection and proof of causality, it is our view that the wider view encouraged by Systems Thinking should at least be considered – there are too many examples of government and other policies not having the desired effect or even accentuating the problems that the 'solutions' were meant to resolve.

Where possible, proposed action plans should be evaluated by a small but representative sample of staff who will be involved in their deployment in order to assess which of the possible approaches are likely to be enthusiastically adopted by the staff who will be responsible for the deployment. In doing so, it must be made clear whether the proposed new initiatives are instead of current procedures or in addition to them.

Finally, the deployment of action plans should be monitored and corrective action taken if they are not implemented or fail to have the desired effects.

Scenario 4: Where No Cost-effective Treatments can be Found

Given the rapid changes in technology and fierce international competition, there will be times when it will not be possible to identify cost-effective ways of turning round the present situation, and more radical action will need to be taken. This could range from investment in new plant and equipment and staff training and development, through to the closure of departments or even sites which are loss-making. Redundancies can be debilitating on morale in the rest of the organization; far from being pleased that they have still got their jobs, those who remain in employment can be deeply upset about the impact of redundancy on their former colleagues and may even feel guilty that they were not made redundant too. The way that both 'leavers' and 'stayers' are treated can affect morale for years to come.

Considering and Taking Action

In the two previous chapters we have drawn attention to the need for decisions about the investigation of problems and their diagnosis to be in the hands of appropriate individuals or teams, and the same comment needs to be made about the responsibility for planning and executing. It is to be hoped that the views of trainers and others who may be involved in 'treatments' will have been taken into account when diagnosis is being considered. Otherwise there is the danger that 'treatments' will be impractical or unacceptable.

Indeed a range of issues need to be considered when possible treatments are being considered. These not only include cost and the speed with which the changes can be implemented, but also the extent to which they are congruent with current business plans and policies. For example, a proposed course of action may be at odds with policies which have developed as a result of discussions about 'Employer Branding'. This is not to say that current policies are always correct – sometimes the emergence of problems will be the first sign that the policies need revision.

Other criteria include the impact on staff and customers, the speed with which changes can be made, and cost. In particular, can the cost of 'treatments' be recovered by resolving the problems or even taking productivity to higher levels?

There are practical issues to be considered too. In a large organization, small changes made in one department can have knock-on effects elsewhere in the organization or even for its customers. For example, changes in the specification of solder in a manufacturing process can have expensive consequences when products fail in remote locations years later. So before changes are made the wider consequences do need to be considered and appropriate consultation needs to take place.

Elsewhere we have already expressed concern about the adoption of 'fashionable treatments'. In recent years one such 'treatment' has been outsourcing. What is now clear is that many companies outsourced functions without giving any thought as to the risks involved and how the outsourcing would be managed and controlled. At worst intellectual property has been lost and data protection regulations have been compromised. A problem with fashionable solutions that are also new is that their apparent benefits may cause others to adopt them before systematic evaluation exposes their downsides.

Evaluation

Finally, there is the important issue of follow-up and evaluation, not just regarding the treatment but the series of processes from problem investigation to diagnosis and eventual treatment. Those running the organization need to know whether the whole intervention has been successful and whether the recommended treatments have delivered the anticipated benefits. The individuals involved in the investigation, diagnosis and treatment phases need feedback on the effectiveness of their work too. A pro-forma that can be used for collecting information for evaluation is outlined below:

- The problem was ...

- The impact that it was having was on ...

- Action needed to be taken because ...

- The causes were ...

- The following options were considered ...

- It was decided that the most effective/cost effective option(s) would be ...

- A programme of changes comprising ... were implemented by ...

- Following an initial 'pilot study' the following changes were made ...

- Evaluation took place ... months after the end of the programme. It was found that ...

- The conclusions of a subsequent review were ...

Concluding Comments

This chapter has been about identifying and implementing appropriate treatments. Even when problems have been clearly identified and diagnosed, it is our view that many issues need to be considered in both the choice of remedial or corrective action, and in its subsequent planning and execution.

In the next chapter we discuss the issue of improving organizational fitness, something that is potentially even more complicated than the resolution of some organizational problems.

Chapter 7
Towards Organizational Fitness

So what is Organizational Fitness and why have there been six chapters before we discuss how to move towards it?

One definition of Organizational Fitness states that an organization is fit if it is ready at all times to handle issues or take up opportunities as they arise. This is similar to the idea of a person being in good health and 'ready for action', as opposed to being unfit or in poor health, lethargic and susceptible to various illnesses.

Being free of major problems is an achievement for an organization, but it is no longer enough. In the face of increasing international competition, rapidly changing technologies, and public expectations that their lives will be better than those of their parents, organizations need to identify and develop capabilities and skills so that they can be winners in the areas in which they are competing.

However, before an organization can move towards Organizational Fitness, any serious malfunctions identified in an earlier diagnosis need to be addressed. Just as athletes cannot give of their best if they have even minor injuries or illnesses, organizations cannot develop full fitness until all significant problems have been addressed and resolved.

There is also the question of where to start. At the start of Chapter 4 we listed the four kinds of measures that may indicate problems – measures of behaviour at work, measures of performance at work, measures of the attributes of employees and measures of how people feel about their work. If current measures indicate that there are no major problems, what is to be done next?

One way forward would be to seek an annual improvement in each of the measures, but for those groups that are already doing well this is likely to be progressively more difficult. A second approach might be to encourage all groups to reach the standard of the best, but arguably some account would need to be taken of the resources available to each group and the circumstances in which each is operating.

Just as athletes decide which sports and events are likely to give them the best chances of success, so a group's fitness objectives need to reflect both what an organization needs and what the group itself can offer. The areas in which an organization wishes to excel should be clear from its strategic plan, but in practice it may not be, or what is stated may reflect just one individual's views of what the market needs rather than something that reflects the actual knowledge, skills, abilities and commitment of employees. Equally, there is little point in a group deciding that it will excel at 'innovation', 'cost reduction' or 'customer service' if these aspirations do not fit with those of the organization as a whole. There may need to be some important preliminary work to look at these issues and decide how the organizational and group objectives can best be aligned. In turn this may affect the choice of measures.

Recently much has been written about the need for organizations to be resilient, defined as 'the positive ability of a system or company to adapt itself to the consequences of a catastrophic failure caused by power loss, a fire, a bomb or similar event', or as 'the ability of a [system] to cope with change'. It would clearly help the process of becoming resilient if the organization was free from any 'sickness' and well on the way to being fit. So powerful as the need is for an organization to become resilient the efforts to achieve this should not be put in the way of the organization first becoming really fit. The implications of this assertion is that the processes, outlined in this book, to achieve fitness should be given precedence over those to achieve resilience.

Some current approaches aimed at improving fitness seek to identify and encourage initiatives from staff, sometimes providing a small number of 'internal entrepreneurs' with considerable resources to develop their ideas, such as mentoring from business school staff. In contrast, we are focussing on approaches which potentially increase the engagement and fitness of all staff, the aim being to move as many people as possible from what has been called 'Transactional Engagement' (where employees simply work to a set of activities or targets) to 'Transformational Engagement' where employees contribute to the development and delivery of business strategy, and help to create and sustain customer services.

There are at least five possible ways forward:

- To encourage local dialogue about possible ways of improving fitness.

- To use surveys and audits to obtain additional information.

- To use organizational change to stimulate fitness.

- To adopt a systematic 'Top-down' approach using a combination of methods and measures.

- To adopt a 'Bottom-up' approach, again using a combination of methods and measures.

Encouraging Local Dialogue about Improving Organizational Fitness

In Chapter 2 we suggested that a gentle and inexpensive way forward would be for staff to be asked open questions about what they think of their jobs, listening to their answers and, wherever feasible, making changes in the light of what the staff have said. So an organization might encourage its managers and supervisors to work in this way, perhaps by offering supplementary training to emphasize the importance of the approach. Thought will also have to be given as to how the resulting information can be collated and prioritized and how improvements can be co-ordinated and funded across the organization as a whole.

Using Surveys and Audits to Obtain Additional Information

In this section we give examples of the kinds of surveys and audits which could increase the information available about the four types of measure and thus identify areas where fitness might be improved.

The collection of information from employees was discussed in Chapter 4, and many points made there apply again here. For example, telling people why information is being sought from them is likely to increase their commitment to taking part in the preliminary work and to finding a way forward. So far as confidentiality is concerned, this should again be offered; however, there may be some people who would like their ideas for improvement to be acknowledged.

The main challenge lies in deciding the focus of the surveys and the methods to be used. In our view the initial focus should be broad because it is unlikely that a 'silver bullet' for improving fitness will be found, and that there are likely to be multiple causes and effects. Semi-structured interviews which give interviewers an opportunity to explore issues raised might be preferable to questionnaires in which the focus of replies is likely to reflect the questions asked.

Some relevant data may already exist from exit interviews, annual appraisals and 360° feedback in which each employee is given feedback about his or her behaviour at work from his (or her) line manager, colleagues and subordinates. This raises the further question of whether an organization is collecting sufficient information about the views of employees on a regular basis, and how much attention should be paid to it. Having introduced 360° feedback, one organization took things a step further, directing that the results of such feedback should be taken into account when promotions and other internal appointments were being made.

A second option is to consider the use of attitude and other surveys, usually carried out by external staff because of the expertise required. In recent years such surveys have tended to focus on 'engagement' rather than 'job satisfaction'. Such surveys can be a source of information about the views of employees and can also provide a means of validating the other sources of information on which management decisions about fitness levels and possible areas of improvement are made.

In general there has been a tendency to use such surveys to identify problems, but they can also be used to identify individuals and groups that are held in high regard by others because of their fitness. For example, during one survey carried out at a time of strained industrial relations, there was repeated praise for the company's managing director. One way of improving fitness might be to identify successful managers, understand the reasons for their success and ask them to mentor those whose skills need developing.

A third option is to make use of one or more of the survey methods provided by external organizations, Investors in People and the EFQM (European Foundation for Quality Management) models being two examples. Both models will yield information that relates to some aspects of the four measures and both models involve training an organization's own staff in their use so that the organizations can prepare for assessments and make self-assessments before external assessors are involved. However, the EFQM Excellence Model does involve collecting considerably more information and the likely benefits and costs of this comprehensive approach will need to be assessed.

A fourth option for improving organizational fitness is to make use of survey methods associated with audits and inspections, an approach favoured by the UK and other governments in the management of the education, health, law enforcement and military services. For example, all UK schools and colleges are subject to inspection by the Office for Standards in Education, Children's Services and Skills (Ofsted) – this normally takes place every four years. In contrast, some of the other inspections tend to be ordered because of signs of problems such as unusually high death rates in hospitals.

In the case of Ofsted, the framework used by the inspectors is available so that schools can assess their own performance ahead of the visit of inspectors. Indeed the view is taken that the whole school should be engaged in how to meet the criteria and in this way what can at first sight appear to be a 'Top-down' system can be a vehicle for participation and engagement. Following the inspection and subsequent report, it is normal for a school to implement recommendations unless serious shortcomings are found.

The system has been criticized for many reasons including the assessment framework used, the relatively short time taken, whether sufficient allowances have been made for local circumstances and the experience of the inspectors. However, this needs to be balanced against the need to ensure high educational standards and organizational fitness.

A fifth option is to focus initially on financial and technical standards and then to consider how these can be improved by changes to the 'people systems'. Publicly quoted companies are subject to financial audits, and auditing companies have developed associated consultancy sevices. Other audits and inspections are relatively rare in the UK commercial sector, but commercial organizations will sometimes arrange technical and other audits of specialist departments to verify fitness and other standards.

A sixth option is to carry out an Organization-Wide Survey which focuses on the extent to which all parts of an organization are working together in a co-ordinated way. Evidence about this may be missed in the some of the other approaches which tend to focus on what is happening within work groups. 'Internal communications' are frequently criticised in surveys, and departments within organizations are often said to be 'functional silos'. The implications are discussed further in Chapter 9.

In general we suggest that an organization should be setting its own standards for Organizational Fitness and monitoring these standards too.

Arguably audits are best used occasionally to verify these standards and their regular or repeated use should be discouraged.

Using Organizational Change to Stimulate Organizational Fitness

Some view the imposition of change as a way of improving organizational fitness. This was the case when a very large organization decided to improve its Organizational Fitness by re-organizing, moving from a structure managed through a large number of District Offices to one controlled by nine Regional Boards. It was decided that, as far as possible, posts in the new structure would be filled by senior managers in the key posts in the old structure, but the question arose as to the basis on which the allocations would be made.

It was also decided that all those seeking posts in the new structure should take part in an Assessment Centre Procedure and that external assessors should be involved so that an independent view could be obtained of the abilities and potential of each applicant. Considerable care was taken over the choice of the consulting organization and the organization selected was able to provide trained and experienced assessors with a wide range of qualifications and commercial and management experience. Care was also taken that each applicant was seen by all the assessors and assessed in depth by at least two of them. Following a series of Assessment Centres each accommodating 12 people, the resulting information was added to that already known about each applicant through comprehensive personnel and other records and the preferences that they had expressed for posts in the new organization. Allocation decisions were made by the personnel director.

From the point of view of the managers applying for posts in the new structure, the experience was challenging. The fact that not a single complaint was made about the process indicated that it was seen to be fair to the applicants, while the personnel director also found the additional information helpful. Indeed when, in subsequent years, there were re-organizations elsewhere in the same group, very similar procedures were used for the allocation processes.

A common error is to expect restructuring to change behaviour. In our view this is unlikely to happen automatically, although the leadership skills of managers can be taken into account when appointments are made to the new structure, both by using assessment centre methods and by reviewing recent annual appraisals. It is also possible to offer training in how the new organization is expected to work, stressing the behaviours expected of staff.

However, while some employees relish restructuring and see it as an opportunity to gain further promotion, such radical change can also be resented or even feared by those who are less confident of their abilities. So it is rare for such change to be welcomed by employees as a whole. It could even be the cause of some of the problems described in Chapters 4 to 6.

So while there may be good reasons for restructuring, its inappropriate use can be a 'high-risk' way of improving Organizational Fitness, particularly if little or no account is taken of the behaviours of managers when appointing staff to the new structure.

A 'Top-down' Approach

This approach is similar to the approach to problem solving described in Chapters 4, 5 and 6, using a combination of methods and measures. It might start by a CEO or other top manager directing that an organization will move towards fitness. Initial objectives will need to be determined and agreed, plans developed and deployed, and results monitored and assessed. Finally the initiative will need to be evaluated and decisions taken about whether to initiate further work of a similar kind.

Each stage is now discussed in turn.

Taking the Initiative

The initiative might be taken by a CEO who sees a picture of declining market share, lethargic staff and poorly maintained premises, but it does not have to be. Any concerned individual could 'put their head above the parapet' and start the process of making their part of the organization even more productive and a better place to work.

It is likely that there will be inertia or even resistance. As with people in their personal lives, organizations can become fat and sluggish, tired, rigid and self-centred. And individuals are likely to differ in the extent to which improving fitness interests them. The reaction of some is, 'If it isn't broken, why fix it?'

Deciding on the Initial Objectives

In our view, those wishing to move towards Organizational Fitness must make two basic decisions. First, will the initiative include all the organization's functions and stakeholders including, for example, the views of customers and shareholders, or will it focus on the behaviour, performance, attributes and views of employees? Second, what kinds of fitness are most important if the organization is to be successful?

Where to Start?

A first step might be to set up a 'pilot study' which could be viewed as the first stage of a rolling programme if the initiative proves successful. In turn this raises the question of which group or groups might take part in the initial pilot study. In our view any areas of extreme success or failure should be avoided in the 'pilot study', while any evidence of a wish to improve or participate would be a positive sign.

Information outlined in the four kinds of measure will then need to be collected about each of the selected group(s). In addition to information about the relevance of the work done, changes in headcount and whether standards are being met, there may be relevant information in annual appraisal and other files. Information might also be gathered from the records of any recent 'exit interviews', and the results of any cases taken to industrial tribunals. Trends in labour turnover might also be considered, as might any information about staff development. It may also be appropriate to obtain information from customers and others outside the organization.

Throughout this process we think it important that employees know what is happening and why. Work groups should be given every opportunity to put forward information to demonstrate their fitness so that their achievements can be recognized.

Examination of the Information – Diagnosis

The information collected needs to be analysed to see whether it is sufficient for judgements to be made about the level of organizational fitness in each work group and how the fitness levels might be improved. Too little information may mean that judgments are erroneous and that ill-will is caused because relevant achievements have not been taken into account. Conversely the endless collection and scrutiny of data, sometimes called 'analysis paralysis' needs to be avoided.

PLANNING AND TAKING ACTION

In our view, even if organizational fitness initiatives are initiated on a 'Top-down' basis, they should be run in ways which encourage all employees to think about the contribution that they can make and the information that they could contribute. For example, in time staff should be told the results of initial assessments of fitness, and have the opportunity to contribute to plans for improving the future fitness of their group. Clearly this might be difficult to do in work groups where fitness has been judged to be mediocre and before doing so possible changes will need to be considered. For example, if the behaviour of a group's manager appears to be the cause of the lack of fitness, a key issue will be whether or not the manager may respond to training or mentoring, or whether s/he should be replaced and any training invested in his or her successor.

FOLLOW-UP AND EVALUATION

It is important to track and evaluate what has happened after improving fitness has been implemented. Do fit groups improve further? Do mediocre groups improve? Do the improved levels of fitness benefit the organization as a whole? Can any financial or other values be placed on the benefits and how do these compare with the costs?

The evaluation process should acknowledge that this has been a 'Top-down' initiative and check whether other options may be better. Some may welcome the fact that the CEO or other top manager wants to make things better and welcome too the opportunity to demonstrate their fitness. But others may complain about the lack of opportunity or time to prepare, or say that their level of fitness would have been better had they been given resources requested long ago. As stated in Chapter 2, there is history of conflict between 'treatments' that are development orientated and those that are based on assessments and these tensions may surface.

A 'Bottom-up' Approach

A fifth approach is to place the emphasis on encouraging staff to make their own reviews of fitness, initiate improvements and assess progress.

Any external assessments of fitness would normally be confined to giving recognition for achievements or investigating failures to improve. At first sight this may seem to be a 'back to front' approach. But in some circumstances it can be appropriate and indeed initial self-assessment is encouraged in the Ofsted approach described earlier.

Figure 5.2, 'A framework for organizational diagnosis', may be useful in planning 'Bottom-up' assessments (see page 62).

The techniques listed down the right of the figure can now be regarded as ways of identifying areas in which policies and procedures might be reviewed and 'tweaked' with the aim of increasing organizational fitness. Just as the application of these techniques can add to the fitness of an organization it should be stressed that inept or even over-enthusiastic application can detract from fitness, so a careful balance must be maintained between belief in the usefulness of the technique and their possible side effects. Again the need to achieve balance within an organization rears its head.

The Areas that Might be Improved

It can be seen from Figure 5.2 that the areas that might be improved are:

THE PROVISION OF JOB AND CAREER INFORMATION

By increasing the quantity and quality of information about the jobs they have available, organizations can improve the vocational guidance given to potential applicants and so increase the chances of better, more appropriate people applying. However, those producing careers and other literature should be careful not to raise expectations to unrealistic levels. In particular, school-leavers often expect to be given interesting and responsible tasks on their very first day at work and can be very disappointed when this does not happen.

PERSONNEL SELECTION PROCEDURES

As has been stated and implied throughout this book the quality and appropriateness of the staff making up an organization is crucial to its health. The skilled use of data-gathering techniques such as interviews, psychometric testing, exercises and trial employment all have their place in improving fitness. But again there is a downside. Too precise matching of people to jobs can lead to inflexibility in the workforce and consequent resistance to the inevitable changes required to keep ahead of the competition. Another issue is that too many specialist personnel selectors see their job as predicting the highly successful performers and ignore the fact that selection is a two stage process. The first stage is to eliminate those people who are likely to fail, and only then deciding those who are likely to be highly successful. By not concentrating on what leads to failure, a brilliant applicant may be recruited who subsequently turn outs to be a pain to everyone! For this reason an organization should assess the risk of taking on people with poor employment records; unless the individuals are carefully monitored they could quickly undermine positive working relationships.

THE PROVISION OF OCCUPATIONAL TRAINING

Once the selectors have recruited staff who showed during the selection procedure that they have the potential to do the work, then those responsible for training have the task of helping them to be competent at it. Again, a very wide range of training techniques are available to achieve this, a demanding diagnostic task for the trainers. Just as people can be over-selected for a job, so too can they be over-trained, again leading to inflexibility and resistance to change.

DEVELOPING ENVIRONMENT, EQUIPMENT AND METHODS

The initial work of the nineteenth century pioneers of 'time and motion study' caused misery and mayhem throughout Western industrial practices. Fortunately the techniques have evolved into 'Ergonomics' and 'Total Quality Management' and are now more widely accepted. The basic objective of these techniques remains, finding out how best the job should be done. However, while a specific 'best way' may sometimes need to be imposed for safety or quality reasons, there is the danger of imposing rigidity and knocking out initiative and creativity.

ARRANGING PSYCHOLOGICAL AND SOCIAL WORKING CONDITIONS

These are probably the most crucial techniques for improving organizational fitness. These range from the use of appropriate appraisal and performance management schemes through to leadership training, in all its many guises throughout all levels of the organization. The underpinning component of all these techniques is interpersonal skills. The downside here is the whiff of manipulation that can pervade them. People react badly when they think they are being manipulated.

ALLOCATING REWARDS

When seeking to improve Organizational Fitness, some give priority to getting the reward system right. But this is a real quagmire of techniques, beliefs and prejudices and in some organizations it seems impossible to get it 'right' in everyone's eyes. So the objective here could well be to ensure that no severe unfairness or anomalies exist within an organization's payment and perquisite procedures.

Managing the 'Bottom-up Approach'

Even when used simply to assess the current way of doing things, the 'Bottom-up' approach can be demanding on managers. If employees become engaged in the review process, searching questions may be asked about current policies and practices and suggestions made for radical and costly improvements. So when seeking suggestions, managers may wish to make it clear that it may not be possible to evaluate and implement all the suggestions made. They may also wish to give some guidance about areas in which ideas will be welcome and whether time and money might be available to research possible improvements.

Such guidance, and procedures for evaluating suggestions, may be particularly important if, for example, and organization lacks new products and services, and efforts are made to identify and encourage 'internal entrepreneurs'. Training may be offered to stimulate ideas. However, the ideas that are produced may require time consuming and costly evaluation let alone huge resources if they are then implemented. In extreme cases they may raise fundamental questions about the competencies of an organization and the markets in which it might best be operating. Without careful management, 'Bottom-up' initiatives introduced with the aim of improving fitness may actually cause tensions and disarray.

Where to Start?

The above analysis is all well and good, but the key issues remain, how to decide which of these techniques should be applied next, how to involve the staff so that there is a high level of commitment towards applying the new 'fitness regime', but as always, it's the first step that is crucial, the initial trigger. By involving members of work groups and discussing options with them, it should be possible to identify 'quick fixes' which enable relationships to be built before the potentially difficult areas are addressed.

Ways in which people in different rôles can support initiatives aimed at increasing fitness are described in the following five sections.

How a Line Manager can Improve the Fitness of a Group

From what has been said in earlier chapters, ways of improving fitness can be divided into two groups – the structural and the behavioural. In our view it is important that a manager should be aware of the crucial differences of these two approaches and to consider the easier and cheaper, behavioural methods first.

A line manager should spend time finding out what is really going on and getting at least some appreciation of the attitudes, views and behaviours of the people in the group. While managers may hope that staff will share their views and values, this is seldom the case. It may be helpful to hold at least some meetings so as to observe and appreciate the dynamics of the group. Who are the people that tend to command respect and influence others? Who the people who say little and tend to be ignored when they do speak? Of course there may be circumstances in which the behaviour of some individuals is likely to be so disruptive that they cannot be included in meetings and decisions about their future in the group may need to be made. The process set out in Figure 5.3, 'A diagnostic model for people management', would be helpful here.

Then when the manager feels that he or she has sufficient knowledge of the group's work, productivity and the attitudes of the group members, it might be worth starting discussions with at least some group members about how the fitness of the group might be improved. What many supervisors can find demanding is finding a way of melding the targets and other demands made by the organization with the aspirations, needs and personal circumstances of employees and some may need mentoring or other training to help them to achieve this.

It can be important to reflect on the management structure of the group in two ways. First, is responsibility divided in ways that make sense to the group's members and to the group's internal and external customers? A simple test is whether or not most enquiries find their way immediately to the person responsible for that activity or whether enquiries go unanswered because no one knows who should be dealing with them. The second issue to consider is whether the right people are occupying the posts of responsibility within the group. If the group leader is to have effective support, then the people in the posts of responsibility must not only be technically competent and able to manage staff that report to them, but must also share the manager's quest for improving Organizational Fitness. Importantly, the manager must be willing to adjust his (or her) views and priorities in the light of the views of staff whose loyalty and commitment is being sought.

How a Human Resources Professional can Improve the Fitness of a Group

There are many ways in which an HR professional can contribute to organizational fitness including the following:

- By the skilled application of the techniques listed in Figure 5.2, 'A framework for organizational diagnosis', and by training managers in their use to help them to meet their targets.

- Ensuring that those recruited and promoted will not only have the knowledge, skills and abilities to perform well in their new post but also the desire to further develop their job-related knowledge skills and to help to make the organization better, also to ensure that those appointed to more senior posts have a track record of success which includes assessing and improving levels of organizational fitness. This is critical – it has been estimated that well-managed groups can be up to 10 times more productive than those which are poorly managed, and no amount of training and development can raise the performance of managers who have significant shortcomings in the abilities, skills and motivation essential for success.

- Arranging training for line and other managers in Developing, Implementing and Evaluating Organizational Fitness Programmes.

- Arranging appropriate professional development and other opportunities for staff to 'benchmark' their knowledge and skills outside the organization and thus keep their part of the organization up-to-date.

- Co-ordinating the deployment of change programmes within the organization, including those aimed at improving organizational fitness.

- Reminding all staff of their obligations as members of an organization and the contribution that each should make to its performance and reputation by 'pulling together'.

How 'Consultants' can Improve the Fitness of a Group

By 'consultant' we mean someone who is not working as a group member. Thus a 'consultant' can be an internal consultant from another part of the organization, or an external consultant, perhaps working for a consultancy organization or independently. Interim managers and other contract staff should be considered.

There are two main reasons for considering the use of a consultant. One is that those seeking to improve fitness lack expertise in some of the related areas. Such expertise may be in technical areas such as the conduct of attitude surveys, project management or in the design of work and working conditions including the use of the latest technologies. But it can also be in the areas of management and leadership where current managers need mentoring and other support.

The second main reason is that the organization simply does not have sufficient numbers of staff in specialized backgrounds at a time when efforts are being made to improve organizational fitness in addition to the day-to-day work of the organization.

However, just as there can be 'pros and cons' about whether to involve consultants in diagnostic work (see Chapter 4) there are issues to consider when their involvement in organizational fitness is being considered. One issue is the size of the fees required by some consultants. Together with the persuasive skills that some high-cost consultants often possess, there can then be tremendous pressure to implement their recommendations as quickly as possible. This may meet the needs of an organization seeking to improve fitness by imposing 'Top-down' recommendations, but may actually make things worse in organizations trying to engage staff through a 'Bottom-up' approach.

A second reason to be cautious is that some organizations lack the technical expertise to assess the costly technical and other recommendations made by some consultants. An example in the UK has been the huge costs invested and wasted in information technology in the National Health Service and other organizations ultimately managed by politicians and their government departments.

So essentially we advise starting with a 'job description' and a view about whether quick recommendations are sought or long-term assistance is required. If the former, the use of consultants may be appropriate, but if the latter it may be better to seek help from interim or contract staff. In contrast we would be wary of any 'consultant' simply claiming that they can offer knowledge, skills or processes that will improve the group's fitness beyond the current levels. Unless the consultant has had access to the results of any preliminary work and can demonstrate a track-record of improving fitness in the relevant areas, we would urge caution.

Staffing Organizational Fitness Initiatives

Although an organizational fitness programme may be initiated by a Chief Executive, s/he is unlikely to be involved in the detail of the work to be done. So a senior manager might be charged with taking an overview of the approaches to Organizational Fitness outlined at the start of this chapter and monitoring their use and effectiveness in practice. Most of the approaches could co-exist in an organization, though not within the same work-group at the same time.

ENCOURAGING LOCAL DIALOGUE

This initiative might be started by identifying rôle-models among current managers and encouraging them to be mentors or even tutors. Then other managers and supervisors might be asked to volunteer as those who will be aiming to improve local dialogue, and induction training provided. This might include recorded rôle-plays so that each volunteer might be given feedback about their style and how it might be changed to optimize engagement. Then, as volunteers engage with their staff, mentoring might be available on request.

SURVEYS AND AUDITS

A key decision is whether to use an 'off the shelf' approach, or whether an approach is to be 'tailor made' to meet the needs of the organization. If the latter, who is to design it and then collect data and arrange 'feedback' for the managers who participate?

Further, an essential part of the approach is that managers and others should be helped to understand which behaviours are likely to yield positive results, perhaps while attending seminars or workshops.

Again, volunteers might be sought in the first instance, although participation could become compulsory over time if results justify it.

ORGANIZATIONAL CHANGE

Although a potentially costly and high-risk approach, there may be occasions when the use of this approach should be considered. For example, a new manager may come to the view that the majority of existing staff have failed to keep up with technical and other changes and need to be replaced.

Decisions will need to be made about how people will be appointed to posts in the new structure and subsequently developed and trained, these might include assessment centre methods involving independent assessors. The options and support available to current employees who are not offered posts in the new structure must be considered too.

THE 'TOP-DOWN' APPROACH

The methodology for this approach will need to be developed so that there is agreement about what performance and other measures are to be used. Self-assessment might be encouraged in the first instance and managers who volunteer should be told about the information that will be collected about the work groups that they manage and why. People will need to be identified who can collect data and interview employees as appropriate, as will those who can assist with the subsequent diagnostic processes and evaluation of possible treatments. When the diagnostic team reviews the information collected about a work group, it is suggested that the group's line-manager should normally have the opportunity to contribute to the discussions of both what the information has revealed about the current levels of fitness and about possible ways of improving them.

Because this approach has much in common with the approach to problem solving described in Chapters 4, 5 and 6, we suggest that the same person (or people) should be involved in the management of both schemes.

THE 'BOTTOM-UP' APPROACH

This approach places more emphasis on giving managers an understanding of what might affect organizational fitness. So it may begin with a series of workshops at which there is discussion of the activities detailed in Figure 5.2 and exactly how managers might take stock of current policies and practices in each of these areas.

Decisions will need to be made about whether and how any independent assessments might eventually take place. One possibility is that they might be carried out as a 'peer review' by other managers, again with the emphasis on development rather than assessment.

If staff invest a lot of time and effort into ideas which are rejected, they are likely to be demoralised. So they should be advised as to whether they might best aim to do things better, to do new things, or both. They might also be given guidance as to how much time and money might be made available to develop, evaluate and implement their ideas.

The Long-term Management of a Fitness Programme

A view will need to be taken as to whether the pilot study or other initial programme has been successful. Not only does account need to be taken of whether specific aims and objectives have been met, but any additional benefits or unforeseen problems need to be considered too.

People vary greatly in their motivation to work and it would be surprising if any initiative succeeded in engaging every employee. Anecdotal evidence suggests that around a third of employees will respond positively to the need for change, a third will go along with it, and a third will fail to raise their game or even resist. Much will depend on how change is introduced and managed, but difficult decisions may need to be taken about those who do not respond positively. However, what can happen is that some will realise that they no longer 'fit in' and may decide that the time has come to move on.

If the overall view is that the first steps have been a success, the question arises as to whether a programme of similar initiatives might follow and how the programme might best be managed. An obvious way forward is to appoint a specialist senior manager with suitable abilities, skills and experience to run the programme. In a medium or large organization, that individual may need some support staff.

When discussing the diagnosis of problems earlier in this book, we cautioned against the automatic and detailed involvement of top staff on the grounds that they may have caused the problems or at least have contributed to them. Further, organizational fitness depends not only on the fitness of individual groups, but how well they work together.

So other options for management should be considered. For example, an Organizational Fitness Committee, comprising senior staff from each of the organization's major functions might be formed to develop expertise in the diagnosis and treatment of problems and the introduction of initiatives to promote fitness. Such a committee might report to a specialist senior manager or to a board member.

However, there is further question as to whether the overall management of problem diagnosis and fitness should be separated from other aspects of change management such as deployment. This is discussed further in Chapter 9.

Funding Fitness Initiatives

Initiatives of this kind will clearly cost money which is difficult to find if budgets are exhausted and economic times are hard. But the costs of some ways of improving organizational fitness are relatively low. For example, it can be seen above that initiatives that involve changing the behaviour of managers and supervisors may involve relatively few costs – the costs may be to do with training people to manage staff better, or to do with changing the sorts of people who are appointed to supervisory posts.

Concluding Comments

In this chapter we have identified a number of ways of improving organizational fitness. They not only differ in the time they demand and cost, but also in the extent to which the engagement of staff is encouraged.

For this reason, before announcing an ambitious Organizational Fitness Programme and perhaps recruiting and training staff, a more modest start might be made. Experience shows that the first steps in resolving problems, in increasing organizational fitness, or in identifying 'competitive edges' nearly always involve winning the support of management and supervision and getting them as a group to display the kinds of behaviours that will get the best out of staff. So for this reason we favour approaches which allow able and motivated staff to contribute to the design and implementation of schemes aimed at improving Organizational Fitness where they work.

Research shows that it is the behaviour of managers, particularly their verbal behaviour, that can encourage behaviours associated with fitness. What then needs to be established are vehicles for such verbal behaviour to take place. It can start with managers walking through their departments and talking with their staff, so-called 'management-by-walking-about', MBWA. Then there are briefing meetings with groups of staff at set times, often at the start of a working day, then there are 'chats', in the corridors, car parks and other convenient places! All such interactions, if they are based on the skilful use of open and probing questions, are highly beneficial to organizational health. The great thing about them is that they have an immediate positive effect and they are the least expensive form of organizational development. It is for this reason that we see leadership as the first key to organizational fitness and why it is the subject of the next chapter of this book.

However, ask managers and supervisors for their views about what would improve organizational fitness and you may get a very different view. For many it is the numerous demands that the organization makes on their time that saps their energy and the effort that they can give to improving fitness in their work groups. Their frustration is increased whenever changes are imposed without consultation and reflect poor internal communications. This is discussed further in Chapter 9.

Chapter 8
Leadership – The First Key to Organizational Fitness

Although briefly mentioned in Chapter 3, the word 'leadership' has been noticeably absent in this book. It is one of the most slippery concepts in the field of management. Even though a great deal of research effort has been put into it, it is still elusive to understand and difficult to define. Senior Managers and CEO's can be seen to fail their organization and cause untold unhappiness and sickness because it can be said that they either lack 'leadership', or have an excess of leadership traits resulting in a style that is dictatorial or even tyrannical. It would be an easy answer to all organizational health problems to prescribe a dose of 'leadership'. But what on earth does this mean *exactly*?

Despite all the research, all the books in business school libraries and the popular management paperbacks piled up at airport bookshops, we are still a long way off consensus as to the exact nature of leadership. There would appear to be a strong tendency to regard leadership as a 'thing', just waiting for a psychologist to discover exactly what it is or a sociologist to find out where it is! This is perhaps comparable to earlier atomic research, it was known that there must be something making up matter and it needed some serious research effort to find out exactly what it was. When this was mainly achieved enormous practical results followed, sadly some of them very unpleasant. One gets the impression that much of current leadership research is set on this course and with similar outcomes possible, a universal panacea for all management (cf. energy) problems, or disaster for the world!

There is also a strong tendency to regard leadership as a *single thing*. Probably made up of many components but somehow coming together, like a Christmas pudding, into a magnificent object to be experienced and admired. Consequently, it is also seen as a *good thing*, unless it is applied by unscrupulous or evil manipulators. Nevertheless it is a widespread belief that individuals, organizations, and even governments, need more of it, as long as it is of the benign kind!

This approach to trying to understand leadership is misguided. Just because leadership can be observed when it is present and noticed when it is absent it cannot necessarily be given the status of an object. It cannot be touched, measured, stored or bought. In these respects it is similar to a rainbow. It can be seen in many variations, according to the situation, admired and regretted at its passing. As there are many different kinds of rainbow so too there are many kinds of leadership. There has existed for a long time the famous four-way classification of leadership styles, 'authoritarian', 'democratic', 'participative' and 'laissez faire' or 'tells', 'sells', 'consults' and 'joins' with the later addition of the infamous WIB – 'weak, inconsistent brute'! There is also the nine-box grid and all its derivatives, that started with 'concern for the task' and 'concern for people', moved into 'transformational' and 'transactional' and proliferated into a massive consultancy and publishing industry. Despite all this commercial effort, an important piece of research yet to be done is to derive a comprehensive and precise classification of the different kinds of leadership rôles that would aid the understanding of what leadership entails.

In Chapter 3 we suggested that what successful managers have in common are the abilities to diagnose what should be done or changed next in order to resolve problems or improve fitness. Elements within leadership may also include strategic planning for the organization as a whole, operational planning for a division, department or section, the delivery of products and services and liaison with functional specialists as appropriate. However, we have deliberately used the term 'leader' (rather than 'manager') because all leaders have followers, however enthusiastic or reluctant they may be. It is this aspect of leadership on which we wish to focus attention.

It would then be extremely fruitful to discover if there was a common core to all leadership activity that all leaders have to be or be able to do. Alternatively, it may be that situations and followers are so different that there is a range of leadership behaviours that are specific to particular situations, such as in an 'emerging economy' or 'new technology' and none applicable to all. The resolution of this issue, perhaps beyond all others, would help us to progress our understanding of the nature of leadership.

Many of the greatest components of human life can also be described as 'rainbow concepts'. Love, beauty, freedom and even motivation, intelligence and personality are all highly valued, admired when present and deeply missed when absent. What they, and leadership, all have in common with a rainbow is that they are an outcome of interactions. We now know that a rainbow is light interacting with droplets of water. Get the angle of interaction right and a rainbow is seen and as we understand the nature of light and the function of prisms, we can explain a rainbow. But how about love, beauty, freedom and leadership? They are interactions between people; and people and situations. So to explain them we need to understand what is inside people and the situations in which they find themselves. A great deal of useful work has already been done on leaders' and followers' traits and qualities, that is, their capacities, inclinations, values and needs. A fair amount has been done too on different leadership situations, for example, military, government and business. What is in short supply is work on the interactions, the process that pulls these components together, that is, research towards a model or a process that would enable us to get the interactions right. One of the major flaws in many of the current process descriptions of leadership is bringing purpose into the model. It is difficult enough trying to describe and explain the process without trying to tie it into the achievement of certain objectives. The tools and techniques of any task can be studied and taught to be carried out correctly without recourse to their ultimate use. How they are then put together into a craft or a game is another, separate, issue. Perhaps the study of purpose can be left to the management theorists and the process of leadership to the empiricists!

So where does this analysis lead us? An approach to the problem of getting the interactions between people and situations right has been lurking in the literature for decades but its complexity and power has not been generally recognized. Rainbows are relatively simple interactions and lend themselves to a simple explanation. Also in human life there are other, complex, interactions that are also admired and valued. Such as those between people and tools, musical instruments and even balls! These interactions are called 'skills', graded sequences of actions where timing is more important than time taken. There is a large body of research findings on the nature of skills and how they can be inculcated. The management literature abounds with references to skills. There are many books on management with 'skills' in their title. They are mainly collections of techniques that effective managers need to be able to do and would provide a useful foundation on which the more complex skill of leadership could be built. It is the main point of this chapter that it is about time that really serious research effort is put into the theoretical and practical implications of defining leadership as nothing more, nor less, than a magnificent human skill.

So what needs to be done? All skills are made up of three components:

- Cognitive.

- Perceptual.

- Motor.

The leadership literature displays that a considerable amount of research has been done on the *cognitive*, that is, what a leader needs to know or even be! A fair amount has been done on the *perceptual*, that is, what a leader needs to see, hear, sense, have 'vision' with different kinds of followers in different kinds of situations. However relatively little systematic work has been done on the *motor*, how a leader behaves, sounds and looks. These are the so-called 'micro-processes' of leadership and are a neglected field, but for some notable exceptions, by both researchers and practitioners alike. The question needs to be raised, why the neglect?

Perhaps one explanation is market forces. Managers who aspire to be called leaders appear to prefer a quick fix, a secret formula or a magic potion. The suggestion that the key lays within themselves and they would have to spend as much time and effort on it as many of them do learning how to interact with a golf ball or a yacht is not to their liking. Many senior managers have been heard to say that they would not be in the position that they are if they did not have sufficient of this skill already. This is sad, as skills, *learning how*, unlike knowledge, *learning about*, can only be acquired by people who want to acquire them and they can only be acquired over time with the help of coaches. Skills training is time-consuming, expensive and labour intensive. So, as was pointed out earlier, a person really has to *want* to become an effective leader if they are going to expose themselves to the self-awareness and feedback that it requires. Hence the unattractiveness of this 'skills approach' in leadership to managers, academic researchers and business schools.

Are there other reasons why a skills approach to leadership is so unpopular? It has been around for a long time in one form or another. Is it naïve? Too simplistic? Too technical? Unexciting? Too threatening? It is certainly not what the market wants. Nevertheless it appears to have the potential to pull together a great deal of the more significant research findings, at least to illuminate the complexity of a very elusive concept. Further, by using the existing research base on the nature of skills, it provides a solid theoretical and practical foundation on which to build leadership training. The abstract concepts of leadership, such as trust, adaptability, balance and alignment, can be attacked by the established techniques of skills analysis. Although far more difficult than analysing routine tasks or even the swing of a golf club, the exercise would nevertheless establish whether or not such notions have any real claim to existence. What would be established is a catalogue of essential behaviours for leaders that would be trainable. Those that were critical but not trainable would then be the province of the management selector rather than the leadership developer. The elusive solid core, the essential components, of all leadership is beginning to emerge from taking this approach. Work at Bradford University suggests that this may be made up of the verbal behaviour that is described later in this chapter. Such a 'micro-approach' does not deny the relevance to leadership of the more 'macro-concepts' of *qualities* and *purposes*, but it does move the emphasis away from discussions of the abstract to considerations of the trainable.

Leadership as a Skill

At Bradford University, once researchers had observed, recorded and studied the audio tapes of a hundred or so managers practising appraisal interviewing, from heads of working groups to the managing director of Fisons the fertilizer company that was, it struck them that what they were studying was nothing more nor less than a complex human skill. All human skills are purposeful, graded sequences of actions between a person and an object such as a ball, a musical instrument, a tool or another person. Conducting an appraisal interview was exactly this. The purpose was changing the behaviour of the interviewee, and even the behaviour of the manager and the organization, just as a skilled musician changes the behaviour of a silent instrument and a quiet concert hall into glorious sound! The key objective of the appraisal interviewer was clear; the person being appraised should leave the interaction able and willing to do their job better. It is a small conceptual leap to realise that this is exactly one of the crucial, if not *the* crucial, indicator of effective leadership behaviour. As was argued in Chapter 5, if as an outcome of interacting with their manager each and every member of an organization became better at their job and at working with others, the results of this would soon be reflected in the balance sheet or in league tables and ratings and the organization would be spoken of as well-managed and displaying the existence of effective leadership and being a healthy organization. Following this observation we renamed the revised edition of the book describing all this earlier work, written with the Fisons training staff, *Staff Appraisal: A First Step to Effective Leadership*.

An appraisal interview can be an enjoyable experience for both the appraiser and the appraisee when both agree that the appraisee has had a good year and deserves the maximum bonus and immediate promotion. Indeed, provided both parties agree that the appraisee's performance is at least acceptable, it can still be a reasonable experience. But it can be very demanding of the manager's skills if s/he considers the appraisee's performance to be unacceptable and even more demanding if the appraisee does not share that view. At worst there can be disappointment about performance and associated ratings, about bonus and about prospects. In many organizations an unfavourable annual appraisal is viewed as being the first step towards dismissal. Not only are the consequences potentially demanding for the employee and his/her family, but they can be upsetting for the employee's manager and colleagues too.

It is easy to say that managers should not allow employee's to build unrealistic views prior to the appraisal interview, but some employees can be coping with terminal illness and other dire situations in their lives outside work and this may have been affecting their performance at work; some schemes make no allowance for this. On the other hand some employees can be excessively full of self-confidence and self-justification and there are tactics that they can use at an appraisal interview which even skilled managers can find difficult to deal with. As well as using extremes of emotion (such as sulking, crying or shouting), tactics can include the following:

- 'Broken record' – saying what they want over and over again.

- 'Fogging' – acknowledging that while there may be some truth in the manager's point of view, the employee remains the better judge.

- 'Negative assertion' – quickly agreeing with criticism so as to lessen its importance.

So while skilled managers with good staff see appraisals as an opportunity to thank their staff for their performance and to reward them with recommendations for bonuses, personal development and promotion, other managers see the whole exercise as something which raises unresolved tensions among staff where relationships are already poor. They can see no benefit in doing it and often do their best to avoid it.

But if people in an organization are not meeting their targets (and it would be surprising if some did not) they cannot be ignored, particularly if the organization aspires to be fit. Managers need to be trained and supported if they are to deal effectively with such challenging situations and in our view this training will also be helpful to them in other aspects of their work. Training methods are discussed later in this Chapter.

Defining leadership as a skill has many practical implications. Skills can only be acquired by people who want to acquire them. And they can only be acquired by personal practice with feedback from a coach or tutor. Watching a video or another person may be a necessary but is certainly not a sufficient way to acquire them. Then they can only be acquired by practice over time. It may come easier to some people because of some natural aptitudes (and it is precisely defining these that is the focus of leadership potential research) but even for those gifted people further practice is always required to realise their potential. But practice by itself is not sufficient. For skill to be developed it has to be with feedback about the effects and effectiveness of the actions. If the practitioners are capable then self-feedback is possible, but having a coach or a tutor, as every serious sportsperson or musician knows, is by far the better way to obtain insightful and powerful feedback.

The Verbal Behaviour of Leaders

Further research, at Bradford, based on more observations and analysis of both audio and video tapes from managers in a wide range of companies and work organizations showed clearly that it is what managers actually *say* when interacting with their staff that is crucial in achieving their objectives and this includes what they write in memos and emails as well. How it is said is also important, but unless this non-verbal behaviour is outside the range of what is usually socially acceptable it is the verbal behaviour of the managers that determines whether or not they will be seen as an effective leader. Further analysis displayed that this verbal behaviour can be grouped into four components: gathering information, giving information, influencing behavior, handling emotion, and all of these can be achieved by the appropriate use of questions and statements.

This can sound simple and obvious, but this is often the outcome of scientific research. It is frequently said that research in the behavioural sciences is making more precise what most people know already and few would dispute that! It is the implications of these findings that are complex and important. When observing and listening to managers interacting with their staff, the effects and effectiveness of different kinds of questions soon becomes very apparent. As was pointed out earlier, much has been written about styles of leadership, most of it is not very useful for management development. However, when the different kinds of questions used in managerial interactions are counted, it is quickly noticed that a relationship exists between:

- *Open questions* and democratic/participative/transformational leadership.

- *Probing questions* and concerned leadership.

- *Closed questions* and detached/task-centred/transactional leadership.

- *Leading questions* and authoritarian leadership.

- *Reflective questions* and person-centred leadership.

- *Multiple questions* and inept leadership.

All these types of questions have their uses and a manager who aspires to be a leader needs to be skilful with each of them and to be able to identify the different situations where each should be used. As has been said and implied throughout the book the skilful use of open and probing questions is crucial for achieving good communications, engagement, empowerment and job satisfaction. But there are situations where they would be inappropriate. Employees who are deeply upset about what is happening to them at work, or with personal problems, may become more upset if asked open and probing questions about their misery and may respond better to gentle reflectives. Then employees who are being difficult and resistant to change may need to be confronted with closed and leading questions that get them to explain and justify their behaviour and attitude and tell them what they have to do differently. Questions beginning with 'you', such as 'you do understand the importance of doing your job this way, don't you?' are central to the authoritarian's way of managing, if they are elegantly constructed and well enunciated they can be very powerful and useful. There is a niche market here for training those managers who are found to be 'too soft' in how to be more authoritarian!

However if authoritarianism is rampant within an organization and is seen as a major source of organizational ill-health and is diagnosed to be reduced and 'engagement' increased, a 'treatment' would be to decrease the proportion of leading questions used by managers when interacting with their staff and increase the proportion of open ones. This is rather easier said than done, old habits die hard and there are also cultural complications. In societies where authoritarianism is the custom members of staff may feel very uncomfortable when asked open questions rather than the closed and leading questions that they have grown to accept. But what is the alternative for changing the managerial style of an organization and even a whole culture? Also, what is the starting point for turning an ailing organization into a healthy one? Working on how managers talk with their staff is a relatively painless way to administer a 'dose of leadership' to start the process of organizational change. Many organizations have suffered the disruptive and highly expensive work of the great firms of consultants who have been commissioned to bring about organizational change and, hopefully, development, usually with massive restructuring and often to no avail. The application of interpersonal skill, at all levels, may well be a less brutal way to bring about changes that result in higher productivity and greater job satisfaction, the signs of a healthy organization.

Verbal Behaviour and Group Leadership

Further research at Bradford University, this time at the group level, found that for a working group to be effective its leader had to balance the four dimensions of working group processes: goal-setting, problem solving, participating, supporting, by using appropriate verbal behaviour. The successful groups in this study, in terms of both their achievement of work objectives and the satisfaction members of the group gained from their team membership, were those where the leaders used their verbal skills to gain roughly equal proportions of questions and statements amongst those four dimensions through using their own contributions to the discussions. Again, this finding is not too surprising as some kind of balance is an essential component of all skills. What this study showed was exactly what it was that needed to be balanced and how such a balance could be brought about.

The task of obtaining balance in an organization amongst all the conflicting needs of the stakeholders is an under-researched area of organizational management. It starts with discovering what members of an organization think and feel through meetings, surveys and just by listening and observing when walking about. Then taking in all this information and diagnosing what needs to be changed *next* to keep the organization in some kind of balance. Like walking a tight rope across Niagara Falls, not an easy thing to do!

The macro skills of senior leaders required to achieve balance, coordination and equilibrium between the demands of groups and the allocation of resources can be set out in the same way as the micro skills. The three components of 'cognitive, perception and motor', and the four processes of 'collecting information, giving information, changing behaviour and handling emotion' apply to all levels of management, but with extra layers of content and complexity the more senior the manager becomes. Senior leaders of work organizations have at their disposal teams of experts and specialists feeding information, but again they have to ask the right questions to be researched by their 'backroom' staff. Then they have assistants and public relations specialists putting out their analysis of the state of the organization and what should be done about it on their behalf. They still have the final responsibility for their decisions, but again there are around them various committees where they can try them out with the ultimate sounding board of a board of directors. However, many of their decisions will cause upset and even anger with the people they bear upon, employees, colleagues, clients, shareholders and sometimes the wider public. It is then that the skill of handling emotion comes into play, from face-to-face with a disgruntled colleague or an aggressive television interviewer to tetchy members of a parliamentary committee. So along with skill of the basic open questions and probes, these are also the crucial interpersonal skills of a 'macro manager' who is confronted by a highly skilled media interviewer, a daunting occasion for many a CEO! It is not widely known that some will be coached for hours prior to such occasions.

There is a further expectation falling on senior managers. They are often said to need 'vision' to be an effective senior leader. But just what is this? Is it putting forward a view of what the organization should be or achieve in the future. This could be some kind of financial success or standing in society but it could be misguided and lead the organization to disaster. Many leaders of states have put forward world domination as their vision, with doom and disaster all round. Many work organization leaders have put forward corporate world domination, with similar outcomes. So the concept of vision is a dangerous one and needs to be more closely defined and linked to creating and maintaining the health of the organization. As was put forward in Chapter 3, particularly in Figure 3.2, all the components of a work organization have to be balanced if the organization is to achieve its objectives. If the activities implied by the central spine of the figure are in balance the organization will run like a well-oiled machine and display the existence of that other elusive concept, 'motivation'. So a senior leader's primary task is to use all their senses to judge whether or not the organization is in balance and ensure that the next decision they make maintains the stability of that balance. If they get it wrong then imbalance will follow and there will be a decrease in the health of the organization.

Then at an even higher level of complexity they have to look at their organization as a closed system, as set out in Figure 3.1. and sense if all the components of the world of work that impinge upon them are in some kind of 'equilibrium'. As was implied by Figure 5.1 there are many conflicting, often warring, groups in the world of work that if they became unbalanced would upset the whole system's equilibrium. It is achieving balance, coordination and equilibrium within and around the organization that is a key task of a senior leader and requires all their cognitive, perceptual and motor skills to decide what needs to be done next to achieve it. If they do they can be regarded as an effective, even a great, leader.

Non-verbal Behaviours and Skills

Once managers have mastered these verbal techniques they can then go on to use the non-verbal micro-techniques, such as facial expression, tone of voice, eye contact and body movements, to enhance the effectiveness of their verbal behaviour. Much work is being put into this aspect of interpersonal skill. What is emerging is that there are far more cultural differences in non-verbal communication than in verbal and this bedevils cross-cultural management. Studies at Bradford have shown that an open or leading question has the same effect on a member of staff despite the language that is used; this applies to French, German, Bulgarian, Hungarian, Spanish and even Mandarin and Bahasa Malaysia, the languages that we have worked with so far, as long as the simultaneous body movements do not conflict with cultural mores about gestures and non-verbal signals that are regarded as offensive in that society. As many expatriate managers have experienced to their cost using an inappropriate gesture can have severe consequences in their interactions with their staff.

Acquiring and Developing Skills

It cannot be asserted too often that, unlike a concept or a belief, a skill can only be acquired by a person if they want to acquire it. A skill cannot be taught, it can be demonstrated but then it has to be learned. It can be said that if only managers put as much effort into learning how to interact with people as many of them do to learning how to interact with a golf ball then many of our management problems would be less today. The unwillingness to do this, unlike learning golf, may be due to the 'loss of face' that a manager may experience when owning up to needing some further training in how to talk to people. Unless and until the owning up is done, interpersonal skill development and therefore leadership development, will not happen. A start to applying this notion that leadership is a skill in an organization can be made with working on the growth of self-awareness and self-analysis in the managers. This can be done by encouraging them to accept feedback about their interpersonal behaviour from their staff and colleagues or on some kind of 'outward bound' event. Some organizations have found a scheme of formally arranged 'learning partners', from different departments in the organization, to be useful in bringing about the giving and receiving of feedback. This gets around the probable sensitivities of discussing interpersonal behaviour with close colleagues.

A start with formal training can be introduced through a minimum of a two-day highly practical training course involving credible case studies, experienced tutors and audio, and perhaps video, recording equipment. Such a powerful event is required to unfreeze any resistance to learning, clear away old habits and lay a foundation for skill development. This is another explanation of the unpopularity of regarding leadership as a skill. It immediately changes management development from learning *about* to learning *how*, with all the time, expense and difficulties that entails.

A further difficulty is starting at the top of an organization. Less than this leads to middle managers saying that it is all right for them to learn the skill and practice it on their staff, but how about how they themselves are managed? They too want to be managed skilfully. But it is not easy to get the chairman, president, chief executive, managing director, vice-chancellor, head teacher to set aside the minimum of two days that it takes to clear away old habits and lay fresh foundations for interpersonal skill development. It is even more difficult to get them to say that, good as they may be, they still have something to learn about managing people and that they are willing to find out just what that is.

To do this is at least leading by example and should have the effect of unfreezing the rest of managers of the organization from thinking that they know enough about leadership. But the greatest impact will come if top managers subsequently demonstrate a sustained change in their on-the-job behaviour, acknowledge the value of the course and encourage others to attend the training. And if they do lapse, it is important that they think through how they might have handled things better and if possible apologise. Such behaviour can be viewed as an element of 'personal mastery', one of five features of a 'learning organization'.

Leadership as an Outcome

This chapter has implied that defining leadership as a skill is a necessary but not sufficient factor in explaining it. The outcomes of sporting and musical skills can be observed and assessed through winning and audience reactions. The criteria for observing and measuring leadership are far less exact and more subjective and this bedevils all leadership research. The macro indices of economic and organizational success are suspect as people often work well *despite* the leadership they experience or suffer! The micro indices of motivation, productivity, commitment and job satisfaction are notoriously difficult to define, let alone measure. Nevertheless, as pointed out in Chapter 5 and at the beginning of this chapter, the first step to effective leadership is to add to the capacity and inclination of staff in their current job. If, by talking with staff in a purposeful and appropriate, that is, 'skilled', way managers can identify what they and their staff should be doing differently *next* and achieving commitment by both to the action plan that brings it about, then the process of becoming a really skilled leader is underway and this is easier said than done!

Human skills are magnificent things. What could now be achieved through applying the concepts and practice of psycho-motor skill, in all their detail, to the leadership of people? How better the world would be if everyone were managed skilfully! The search by academics for a magic formula for leadership, the crock of gold at the end of the rainbow, will no doubt continue. In parallel, there are a plethora of consultants and trainers offering experiences that are claimed to develop 'leadership' in individuals and organizations in venues ranging from country mansions to windswept hills, with the claims for what they can achieve seemingly quite magical! These events may well be useful for 'unfreezing' managers from their current views of themselves and the nature of management. Whether or not they inculcate the skill of leadership is questionable. There are no short cuts to skill acquisition and, sadly, there are no 'quick fixes', not even reading all the books on leadership currently in the various management publishers' lists. The rather unpopular message of this chapter is that the way ahead is through the somewhat slow, laborious, sometimes painful, growth of skilful interpersonal interaction.

Concluding Comments

Because of the difference that skilled leadership can make and because leaders are also often involved in both the diagnosis and treatment of organizational problems and in raising the standards of organizational fitness, it is our view that skilled leadership is a key element in resolving organizational ills and improving fitness, while unskilled leadership is likely to be the dominant cause of those ills. Further, those who lack these skills are likely to make excessive use of 'Top-down' approaches when diagnosing organizational problems or attempting to improve Organizational Fitness and these approaches may alienate some staff.

Skilled leadership needs to be developed in two key areas. First, managers need to develop good levels of skills in communicating with their staff. This should have the immediate effect of helping them better manage their staff and to conduct appraisal interviews in ways which enhance the enthusiasm and commitment of staff.

Second, it is our view that the better communications will also benefit the identification and resolution of problems described in earlier chapters. There will be an interest in finding out the causes of problems rather than ignoring them or apportioning blame. And there will be a greater willingness to evaluate systematically possible solutions and hopefully identify and discard those options which may actually make things worse.

Skilled leadership is required at all levels in an organization, but particularly by the senior management of an organization where it is crucial for achieving a technically sound, administratively convenient, politically defensible and socially acceptable diagnosis of what an organization should be doing differently *next*. For some employees it is the most important part of an organization's internal communications. And it is internal communications that we see as the second key to Organizational Fitness, which we discuss in the next chapter.

Chapter 9

Internal Communications – The Second Key to Organizational Fitness

Much of this book has advocated systematic approaches to Problem Solving and Improving Organizational Fitness. However, in Chapter 8 we drew attention to aspects of leadership which have been consistently overlooked and which should help improve the fitness of organizations if they are applied.

In this chapter we draw attention to further matters which may not be given sufficient attention, and which may not be apparent if investigations are focussed within work groups. They concern internal communications and co-ordination. This is because Organizational Fitness is not just to do with relationships within groups, but also to do with groups working together. When organization-wide surveys have been carried out, one of the areas most heavily criticized has been 'internal communications'.

Traditionally, internal communications have focussed on the announcement of management conclusions and the assembling of management thinking into messages for mass distribution to 'the troops'. These messages are necessary for keeping staff informed about what is going on in the organization but the importance of getting the content and tone of them appropriate for their purpose is much under-estimated. Frequently they result in staff feeling alienated rather than communicated. Just as Chapter 8 stressed the interpersonal skill required for effective face-to-face interactions further research at Bradford displayed the importance of written skills in communication through memos and e mails and how expressions of concern can aid the acceptance of the message by staff. The key concept of this research was to bring about the staff 'feeling communicated' and to set out the writing skills required to achieve it.

Recently, the term 'employee voice' has been put forward to embrace all the processes and procedures that organizations can use to develop internal communication. There are very many of them, ranging from suggestion schemes, through joint consultation with trade unions to worker directors, all can be seen described in personnel management texts. It is useful to note, much to the pleasure of British trade unions, that internal communication and engagement is at last being recognised and taken seriously by work organizations. Probably helped by the repackaging and giving the processes and procedures a new, all embracing name.

'Top-down' Communications and Deployment

Many university business schools have Professors of Strategy and the importance of developing a good business plan should not be underestimated. However, as yet there are no Professors of Deployment. Does this mean that knowledge and skill are not needed to get things done and to make things happen? Anecdotal evidence suggests not.

In military and other large organizations, the word 'deployment' is used to describe the planning and execution of 'top-down' initiatives. In some there is recognition of the sustained effort required to implement and embed 'top-down' changes, particularly any changes that may ultimately affect every individual in that organization. Indeed those who have worked in large organizations such as the National Health Service, British Telecom, the Post Office and major supermarket chains will almost certainly have experienced some of the problems that can occur. Viewed from the organization's headquarters, it can appear almost impossible to get staff to take notice of changes in processes and procedures, let alone implement them. However, viewed from the bottom of the organization, the deluge of information from headquarters can imply that local staff have nothing else to do other than wait for the latest initiatives to arrive.

Indeed, some local staff will claim that they are the victims of the 'mushroom theory of management' – that for most of the time they are kept in the dark, but from time to time the door opens, the light shines in and they can briefly see what they are doing before someone throws muck over them! Worse still can be the task of trying to change procedures that are inappropriate or ineffective – particularly if those suggesting change are at a remote outpost.

Why do problems with 'Top-down' Deployment keep occurring? First, because some large organizations are accountable to parliament and undertakings given in the heat of parliamentary debate can have huge implications for day-to-day working practices and procedures. Second, because the future careers of some staff based in the headquarters of large organizations seem to depend on the number of initiatives that they can devise, implement and subsequently list on their CV. Indeed such thinking sometimes leads to the investment of huge sums of money in so-called vanity schemes (such as the introduction of massive computer systems into government departments) that require so much money that they jeopardize other services. Third, because some staff working in headquarters (and their political masters) can lack the operational experience to assess the true consequences (and costs) of their promises and actions.

Problems of deployment are not confined to large organizations. Some small business owners are notorious for dreaming up ideas that are way beyond the company's resources and which their staff do not have time nor the financial budgets to implement.

Examples of Problems with 'Top-down' Deployment

Problems with 'Top-down' Deployment are legion. Here are some examples:

- Details of a major training initiative to be deployed at the beginning of January reached the offices of the trainers on Christmas Eve, virtually all the trainers had left for the Christmas break and none planned to return to work until after the initiative had been scheduled to start.

- One large organization introduced several major and related changes on the same day – 1 April 2013 – a day which was also a public holiday when all the administrative offices were closed.

- Staff in a large organization received a leaflet telling them that they could have a sabbatical (a period of time off without pay) and that they should request this from their line manager. Neither line managers nor local human resources staff knew of the initiative and no policies or processes had been agreed. Inevitably, when staff requested a sabbatical, their line managers refused to support the request because alternative trained staff were not available. Far from improving morale, the initiative raised expectations that could not be met and lowered employee satisfaction.

- Proposals were made for the way that the major parts of a large organization should relate to each other in financial and other ways. However, the pages of proposals were so complicated as to be incomprehensible to senior staff, let alone other staff in the organization who would be required to implement or operate them.

- A new computer system allowed junior administrative staff to make unlimited numbers of routine requests directly to doctors rather than to their practice managers, greatly increasing the administrative workload on doctors.

Planning a Successful Deployment

Arguably successful deployment will involve at least some of the following stages.

Ideally there needs to be a good understanding of the situation 'on the ground' among those planning changes. For example, one organization issued instructions that each manager's objectives should be displayed on their desk and threatened disciplinary action against any who did not comply. However, some managers working shifts were sharing the same desks ('hot-desking') while others had no desks at all.

Second, the capacity and capability of staff who will be involved in deployment needs to be considered. This may need to include an assessment of their willingness and ability to learn new things. If necessary, additional training may need to be given and in extreme cases there may need to be policies about what to do with those who cannot absorb the new information.

For example, there has been a trend in British education for head teachers in schools to be given more responsibility and for the controls by local education authorities to be relaxed or even withdrawn. This means that head teachers have been able to sign major contracts with suppliers without seeking advice from specialists – indeed, in some areas the specialists who would have offered such advice have been made redundant. A consequence has been that some head teachers have been victims of a 'scam' involving the supply of computers for classroom and other use. In the belief that the computer equipment was being funded by means of a government grant, they signed contracts with commercial contractors worth millions of pounds. Only later did they discover that the value of the equipment was greatly overstated and that there was no central funding of the costs. The result is that some schools are now in debt for those millions of pounds and a number of head teachers, possibly close to 100, have been required to resign their posts. Police are now investigating this nationwide scam.

Third, capacity needs to be assessed in terms of staff time available to implement treatments or other remedial action. Often proposed changes involve staff doing additional work rather than simplifying or streamlining what they have to do. Elsewhere an example has already been given of how the deployment of a series of training initiatives would have taken up more than the whole working week of the line managers responsible for implementing them.

One way of making initial assessments of capacity and capability would be for large organizations to identify typical hospital wards, retail stores, delivery offices, etc. and then to assess the impact of the treatment or initiative on the staff working there in terms of their workload, their cognitive abilities and their personality and motivation. These could be actual places or sites or even be virtual organizations based on computer models.

Fourth, the implications for deployment should ideally be considered when strategic options are being identified and evaluated. There is otherwise the danger that strategic options will be chosen that are almost impossible for an organization to implement.

Some may feel that this cannot be done in practice – that it would be too time-consuming to collect all the relevant information ahead of every strategic option being discussed. So a practical way forward might be to have a two-stage process in which strategic options are identified and short-listed, and then the implications for deployment are assessed for the stronger options before a final decision is made.

Fifth, initiatives should be 'piloted' in typical or representative areas. This can be particularly important if the other suggested preliminary stages have not taken place. However, such 'piloting' can have limitations. First, the trial sites are sometimes chosen through personal contacts reflecting the known enthusiasm and ambition of the local manager and the staff working there, and reactions may not be typical. Second, the involvement in a new initiative can in itself increase morale and enthusiasm, partly as a result of contact with the consultants or other advisors piloting the scheme and perhaps too because of the visits of top staff interested to learn how the initiative is progressing.

Clearly there is little merit in conducting the first trials of an initiative at places notorious for failure. But there is a case for the further testing and refinement of an initiative at some less compliant locations. This is particularly important if those affected by the deployment are using high value equipment and/or involved with major sales to major customers. Indeed, evaluation should include all those ultimately affected and not just those directly involved in deployment.

Sixth, in an attempt to get attention and create interest, plans for deployment sometimes include the endorsement of a director or other senior member of staff. Indeed some organizations have gone further and have involved a famous sports or other personality to launch a major new initiative. Sometimes plans have included a 'launch' at meetings of senior staff or even a special conference or other meeting for those to be involved in the deployment. In the past such events would have been both time consuming and expensive, but on-line video-conferencing and webinars have opened up new low-cost possibilities.

Seventh, the deployment may require staff to be trained in new skills and in turn this raises the question of whether their attendance, learning or subsequent job performance should be assessed. Records of attendance, etc. may need to be kept. As part of one initiative, first-line managers were required to attend a series of briefings before being assessed. Those who did not meet the required standard were told that they could not continue as supervisors, but were allowed to appeal the decision. At appeal one manager was adamant that he had not been invited to attend any of the briefings, but the attendance records showed otherwise.

Eighth, the progress of deployment needs to be monitored to check that things are going according to plan. If they are not, an assessment needs to be made as to whether to continue with deployment, or whether to revise or even abandon the whole project. In making such a decision, it is again important to have an accurate overview of what is happening 'on the ground'. For example, one scenario may be that the deployment is generally going well with minor delays in one department which can be overcome. This would be totally different to a second scenario where virtually all departments in which deployment has taken place have experienced difficulties and major problems have occurred in some areas.

Difficult decisions can arise when it is becoming clear that 'top-down' changes are running into difficulties. Initially it may seem sensible to push against apparently trivial reasons for not implementing a plan, but at what stage does it become sensible to amend a plan or even scrap it? For example, the UK government is aiming to have all those claiming unemployment and similar benefits do so on-line. Yet 17 per cent of households are not yet on-line and anyone who has tried to help less able people to use computers will know what a difficult and sometimes impossible task it can be.

Finally an overall evaluation of the treatment and its implementation needs to take place, with those responsible for planning understanding where things have gone to plan and where difficulties have been encountered. This experience needs to be recorded and to be accessible to those developing strategies and planning deployment in the future.

'Bottom-up' Communications

There are four reasons why attention might usefully be paid to 'Bottom-up' communications and ways in which it might be improved.

First, organizations should have some knowledge of how things are on the ground. Among other things, this information can be used in the planning of changes.

Second, organizations need to have ways of knowing when things are starting to go wrong, rather than finding things out when a crisis point has been reached, and recovery is difficult if not impossible.

Third, organizations need to know when things are going well. In particular, if problems need to be diagnosed or fitness improved, it can be helpful to be able to compare work-groups where things are going well with those where there are problems. Further, recognition of good performance can also have huge benefits in terms of motivation and morale.

Fourth, those 'on the ground' can sometimes contribute valuable ideas in terms potential savings or even new business ideas. One example concerned Honda whose sales of large motorbikes in America had been poor. A few mopeds had been imported for use by junior staff running routine errands and they noticed that the interest in the mopeds was greater than the interest in the larger bikes. Their observations were relayed to Honda's headquarters in Japan and as a result Honda decided to export mopeds to America. Consequentially, Honda became a market-leader.

It is said that good managers recognise that much of the knowledge required for businesses to be competitive is actually in employees' heads'. However, if this is to be successful, what needs to be recognised is the time and skill demanded of all those in the communications 'chain'. Further, if conflicting demands are being made by those above and below them, middle management may be placed under considerable pressure. To be effective, middle managers will need to be selected and trained with care, and may require additional support when major changes are being proposed, evaluated or implemented.

Communications between Work Groups

Thus far, what has been written is mainly about 'top-down' communications with the suggestion that 'bottom-up' communications might also be reviewed. But what of communications between work-groups, and between work-groups and their customers? These can be an important determinant of Organizational Fitness and are easily missed in studies which only focus on relationships within work groups.

Most organizations have charts which describe their structures, but in spite of these there are numerous examples of the failure of 'Top-down' Deployment. Where are the organization charts that describe the relationships between departments? Where are the surveys and other information to show how effectively departments are working together? Certainly there is much anecdotal evidence of problems such as responsibilities that overlap between departments that can cause conflict and important activities for which no-one has responsibility.

Interestingly, information about whether and how work-groups are co-ordinating their activities is sometimes collected by academic and other researchers, but its potential for wider use has received relatively little attention. An exception comes from the suggestion that managers and their staff could usefully reflect on the ways that orchestras achieve success, each player having his or her own musical score and the conductor coordinating their efforts and establishing priorities. Many organizations would be fitter if individual job descriptions reflected the overall plan without conflicting with each other, if staff knew the part that they and others were expected to play in achieving success, and if the conductor were to co-ordinate their efforts. The analogy is particularly helpful in calling into question the effectiveness of some managers in 'conducting' rôles who keep information to themselves.

The absence of information about the interdependence of work groups can also affect the induction of new staff, and others who need to know how an organization works because they are trying to handle enquiries from customers and other members of the public. Often this is something that new staff have to learn for themselves.

The Case for Co-ordinating Change

It is clear from the above that deployment and other changes require expertise in planning and execution. But is it sufficient for an organization to have such expertise dispersed among its managers or should it be led or co-ordinated in some way?

It is strange that many organizations take enormous care over the scheduling of work for clients and the efficient use of expensive machinery and yet fail to plan and co-ordinate the many demands that they make on managers and supervisors. Thus managers and supervisors can be required to please customers, manage staff, produce business plans and annual budgets, carry out and report staff appraisals, liaise with other departments and then have time to deploy the latest initiatives from head office as well as identify and build on any local initiatives.

What is often missing is any attempt to co-ordinate the demands made on workgroups, be they routine or resulting from initiatives. Such co-ordination would be popular among those who have worked in large organizations and who have been on the receiving end of an endless stream of uncoordinated initiatives and we have already raised the possibility of a real (or virtual) unit being used as a 'model' to help assess the practicality and timing of changes. But how might co-ordination be achieved?

There is unlikely to be a universal solution applicable to all organizations. So a first step must be to get the company's chief executive and directors to take stock of the situation in their organization, perhaps by commissioning an organization-wide survey. Is 'initiative overload' a problem in their organization? How well are departments working together?

So far as 'initiative overload' is concerned, progress may be difficult, because each management function is likely to want to be able to demand information or introduce changes when it suits them. And even if the need for better co-ordination between work groups is accepted, how might this be encouraged in practice? Should an individual, or group of individuals, be given responsibility for approving and prioritizing all changes? Would these 'Fitness Managers' also have the power to assess whether proposed changes are technically sound, administratively convenient, socially acceptable and politically defensible and perhaps reject some of them? Would the 'Fitness Managers' have powers to access and influence budgets to help implement changes? Would they have responsibility for developing, implementing and evaluating a programme of change which can be absorbed into the organization at a realistic rate?

While the Board of Directors or an equivalent group may need to approve major initiatives, there must be a question over whether they should be involved in the scrutiny of each initiative and, if approved, its place in a programme of change. If, as is often the case, the directors meet only occasionally, they do not seem to us to be best placed to consider all proposals or co-ordinating their deployment.

One possibility might be to make a director (or some other top or senior manager) responsible for Fitness Management throughout the organization, in the same way that it has been fashionable to for some organizations to appoint a director of strategy. Indeed, one possibility would be for a director to have responsibility for both functions.

Another person who might have overall responsibility for fitness is the head of human resources/personnel, since that department has responsibility for many of the potential techniques relevant to diagnosis and treatment.

However, some would say that Organizational Fitness is too big and important a task to be left to one person. So another possibility is to share responsibility between a sub-committee of directors, or even to set up an Organizational Fitness Committee comprising senior staff from the departments most likely to be involved. Some will mentally groan at the prospect of a committee, but it could help to improve communication and co-ordination between interested parties and ensure that the programme of work was realistic and achievable.

Finally, there are processes such as those devised by the European Foundation for Quality Management that offer an 'off the shelf' approach that covers some relevant information.

It is clear from the above that there is no simple or obvious answer and this may be why the matter of co-ordination is seldom addressed. But without addressing co-ordination, true fitness cannot be achieved.

Concluding Comments

The achievement of Organizational Fitness depends on resolving any problems and then developing both all-round fitness and particular strengths. But it also depends on successful deployment of new initiatives, and on senior staff being in touch with what is happening 'on the ground'. Co-ordination between work groups also needs to be assessed. There is expertise to be developed in all these areas, and 'know-how' to be developed which could help an organization prosper in an increasingly competitive world.

Chapter 10

The Way Ahead

We hope the message of this book is clear, that organizations should not proceed to change any of their policies, procedures, processes or practices until a systematic thorough diagnosis of the root cause underpinning the need to change has taken place. This need not take a great deal of time nor be expensive as long as it is approached as objectively as possible by the key people involved in and who will be affected by the change. Sometimes what needs to be changed is blindingly obvious, but it will still have to be checked over and discussed. As was set out in Chapters 4 and 7, the staffing of the 'teams' that are designated to make the diagnosis and decide on the treatment is crucial.

As has been pointed out and implied throughout the book, the process of diagnosis that leads to a technically sound, administratively convenient, politically defensible and socially acceptable decision to change an organization in some way is fraught with difficulty. It is hoped that the suggestions made throughout the book will ease this task.

But what is the way ahead? Just as medicine has progressed by doctors sharing information, so it hoped that organizations will start to share their experiences in undertaking diagnoses and applying treatments. Professional institutions could help by being a repository for the information that organizations would be prepared to release, in return for getting information about other organization's efforts. Perhaps too they would write-up and publish their attempts at diagnosis and treatment, or provide facilities to an academic to write-it-up for them, to their mutual benefit. The academics would get data for useful publications and the organizations would get esteem from their various stakeholders for being active in seeking justifiable change and for being open about what they achieved by it. Such publications would undermine the influence that contemporary popular books on management have on encouraging the application of 'quick fixes' and 'fashionable solutions' and demonstrate that organizations should seek their own solutions to becoming fit and great rather than mimicking the apparent elite.

In our view there are three ways of enhancing the whole process of organizational diagnosis and treatment: First, by developing a manual for organizational diagnosis; second, by developing statistically based diagnosis; third, by making training available with the ultimate aim of offering a professional qualification in organizational diagnosis.

Each is discussed in turn.

Towards a 'Manual for Organizational Diagnosis'

So how can such a manual be developed that contains a classification of all organizational ills and the treatments available that would make them fit and healthy? A lead can be gained from what has been done in the field of mental health. If only human resource managers and organizational psychologists had the equivalent of the *Diagnostic and Statistical Manual of Mental Disorders* that exists in clinical psychology, the task of helping organizations to be more effective would be enormously eased. This comprehensive classification of mental disorders is produced by the American Psychiatric Association and is now into its fifth version. Its history is long and its evolution since the first version, DSM-1 in 1952, has been influenced by work of individual practitioners, researchers and academics co-ordinated by the World Health Organization. The 1994 DSM-IV came out of a task force of 13 working groups and over 1,000 psychologists, psychiatrists, statisticians and other professionals from all over the world. In the introduction to this 913-page manual is the cautionary statement:

> *The specified diagnostic criteria for each mental disorder are offered as guidelines for making diagnoses, because it has been demonstrated that the use of such criteria enhances agreement among clinicians and investigators. The proper use of these criteria requires specialised clinical training that provides both a body of knowledge and clinical skills. These diagnostic criteria and the DSM-IV classification of mental disorders reflect a consensus of current formulations of evolving knowledge in our field. They do not encompass, however, all the conditions for which people may be treated or that may be appropriate topics for research efforts. The purpose of DSM-IV is to provide clear descriptions of diagnostic categories in order to enable clinicians and investigators to diagnose, communicate about, study and treat people with various mental disorders.*

A tremendous amount of work has been put into and now considerable controversy has arisen, around the publication of DSM-V. No doubt the clinical psychologists will sort it out! In the meantime organizational psychologists are yet to make a start on MOD-1. This manual could start with a list of 'Signs and Signals of Organizational Sickness and Health' along the lines of Appendix A. Then, as has been said, it could list and categorize all the sicknesses that organizations could suffer from and list and categorize all possible treatments. This manual could also be the depository for all the checklists developed by different types and sizes of organizations so that managers who are concerned about their own organization can have access to the attempts by others to get at the root causes of organizational ills. It will be a great but worthwhile task, hopefully spurred on by the thought that the diagnosis of organizational ills will always be a hit-and-miss, primitive, crude, inexact and painful process until such a manual exists. In the meantime this book has put forward a base on which others can discuss, argue about, and so work towards building a generally available and widely accepted diagnostic scheme for organizational sicknesses.

Chapter 5 demonstrated the complexity and difficulty of getting to the root cause of an organization's problem and this book has stressed that there is no excuse for failing to collect systematically relevant data and attempting an 'enlightened diagnosis' before embarking on any organizational treatment. But here is a stumbling block, how to use the data to go beyond an enlightened diagnosis to achieve an 'evidence-based' diagnosis that can stand up to statistical confidence limits. A tentative attempt towards this will now be attempted.

Towards a Long-term 'Statistical Evidenced-based Diagnosis'

The first step in developing a systems-based statistical procedure for organizational diagnosis is to face up to the realization that there are always multiple causes and multiple effects, as the quotation from J.S. Mill at the opening of this book identified. Consequently the methodology to untangle them and to come to the decision of what change needs to made next to improve the fitness of an organization will have to be 'multivariate analysis'. Fortunately great strides have been made to make these complex statistical techniques more user-friendly. Various packages of computer programmes, notably, 'Statistical Package for the Social Sciences', now known as IBM SPSS, are widely available. A great deal of work is being done in the field of organization modelling and simulation which could lead to sets of decision rules that would help to focus the data analysis onto the probable outcomes of changing an organization. The

School of Computer Science at Nottingham University is at the forefront of this work. They say:

> Systems simulation is becoming increasingly popular as a decision support tool in Operations Research and Management Science. This can be accounted to the recent increase in data availability and improvements of speed in computer hardware. Systems simulation helps to better understand the processes currently in place and shows the consequences of changes to these processes over time. Besides its standard application of studying the operations of a system it has more recently also gained attention as a useful tool for studying the behaviour of people in human centred service systems.

It can be hoped that the Nottingham team (and others, including IBM) will focus some of their efforts on the key methodological issues raised in this book and even carry forward some of the proposals made later in this chapter.

The structure and components of the models given in the previous chapters indicate the kinds of data that would need to be assembled to feed the simulations. As with all large scale statistical analyses, spreadsheets comprising all the variables that could have an effect on what is going on in the organization will have to be set up. The National Health Service (NHS) attempted a well-intentioned but disastrous project to establish a very extensive data base. They already had a considerable amount of data about staff engagement through their annual National Staff Survey which could have been incorporated into the data base to provide a very comprehensive approach to diagnosing all the strengths and weaknesses of the magnificent NHS. Sadly it looks as if the scheme (NPfIT) was too complex and difficult to work and it was scrapped. Various commercial data bases are available on-line. What they appear to lack that would be helpful for making more comprehensive diagnoses are scales of the intervening variables that can be derived from the context within which an organization exists; these need to be presented in the form of options or scales so that features can be recorded and included in the subsequent computer analyses.

To move forward, a database needs to be developed that would contain all the information about the work of the people making up the organization. It would include information about their performance, that is, measures about how effectively the individual is working. These can be 'objective', such as number of things made or sold, or 'subjective', such as supervisors' ratings. A further section is then required listing all the organizational and contextual variables. Again, these can be either 'objective', such as numbers employed, costs, labour-turnover, and 'subjective', such as morale, job satisfaction and a plethora of material from employee surveys. It is to be noted that the scaling of these variables is not critical. Modern multivariate analysis programs can handle all level of scales; ratio, interval, ordinal and nominal.

In the early days of using this methodology to understand what was going on in various sales organizations, one study showed that how far the salesman worked from head office, a ratio level measurement, was associated with high ratings of work performance, those working closest to head office getting the higher ratings. Another study indicated that whether or not the salesman played golf, a nominal variable, (which was scaled 2 for a player, 1 for a non-player) was associated with ratings of performance, the players getting better ratings in a company where most of the top managers were golfers. These findings needed to be explained and the explanation showed just how inadequate the company's performance measurement procedure was. This led to a major revision of the staff appraisal procedures.

Another study of a sales force selling tyres included 'scores' on ability tests and personality profiles. When the results were analysed, much to the surprise of the management, the best salesmen, as measured by their sales performance, that is, value of sales achieved, could be described as 'grey men' as their scores on the questionnaires indicated they were 'humble', 'shy', 'tender-minded' and below average in intelligence for the group. As an explanation the managers suggested that, as they were by no means brand leaders in their market and their products were not widely advertised, the sales technique found to be most effective was for the salesman to 'hang around' the tyre depots hoping to solve some of the supply problems of the depot manager in meeting urgent orders. The company was able to provide a quick service in supplying tyres, being more flexible and centralized than its larger competitors. Consequently the successful salesman in this organization was not an energetic order taker but a quiet self-effacing man who was prepared to get his orders by merging into the background of a depot, rather than by any hard-selling techniques. This finding had very significant implications for the selection and training of salesmen in this company.

As the quotation from Nottingham indicated, the memory size of modern computers, unlike in the early days when the research underpinning these proposals was carried out, now imposes little constraint on how many variables are included in the database. Many commercially available databases are now marketed making this part of the process much more user-friendly.

Consequently organizations are encouraged to 'throw the kitchen sink' into the mix. Not only will surprise results emerge, as exampled above, but confidence in the data will take place when the obvious and expected results are observed.

So the next step is to understand the underpinning theoretical structure of organizational analysis that results in 'theories' explaining what is going on within the organization. Figure 10.1 sets this out showing how a descriptive account of the observed events existing within and around an organization can be used to provide theories explaining them as a precursor to making decisions about possible diagnoses.

Figure 10.1 is a conceptual model of the process involved in analysing and interpreting data. It sets out the classic stages of all scientific and technological

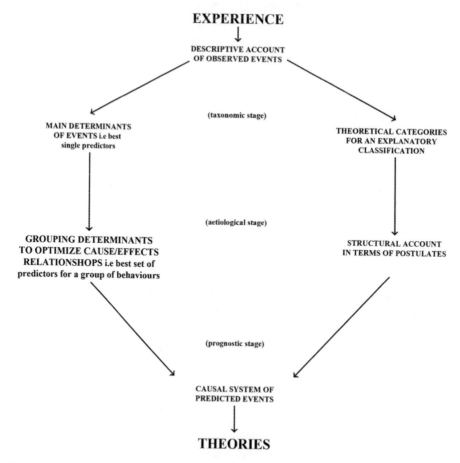

Figure 10.1   Interpreting the results of multivariate analysis

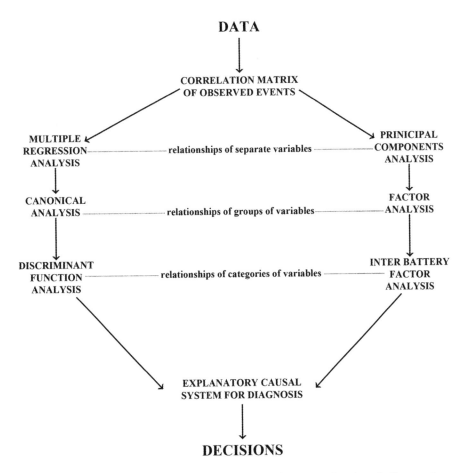

DATA

↓

**CORRELATION MATRIX
OF OBSERVED EVENTS**

**MULTIPLE
REGRESSION** ··········· relationships of separate variables ··········· **PRINICIPAL
COMPONENTS
ANALYSIS** ··· **ANALYSIS**

↓ ↓

**CANONICAL
ANALYSIS** ··········· relationships of groups of variables ··········· **FACTOR
ANALYSIS**

**DISCRIMINANT
FUNCTION** ··········· relationships of categories of variables ··········· **INTER BATTERY
FACTOR
ANALYSIS** **ANALYSIS**

**EXPLANATORY CAUSAL
SYSTEM FOR DIAGNOSIS**

↓

DECISIONS

Figure 10.2   **A multivariate analysis system for organizational diagnosis
– MASOD**

research, science on the right, technology on the left. It starts by assembling data on what is going on in and around an organization. Then deriving a classification of all the events that make up a field of study, the taxonomic stage; second, grouping these determinants into factors that help to explain the causes of these events, the aetiological stage; finally deriving decisions by manipulating the data that would predict what would happen if any of these determinants are changed, the prognostic stage. Hopefully, the result of all this activity is an understanding what is really going on in an organization.

The statistics that can be used to provide meaningful outcomes of the analysis are set out in Figure 10.2 above.

The computer programs for each of these statistical techniques are readily available. However they have yet to be brought together into a user-friendly package that enables an organization to really understand what is going on inside it. Readers of this book who want to follow this advanced path towards diagnosis can use the programs independently, perhaps through IBM SPSS. The output will be a mass of statistics that would provide an organizational diagnostician familiar with such data the opportunity to understand what is really going on in an organization and point towards what should be done next to make it more productive and a better place to work in. This output is equivalent to a whole body scan undertaken by medical diagnosticians and would require an equivalent amount of knowledge and skill to interpret it. They can be termed 'orgscans' and could be the key to organizational diagnosis in the future. The process of analysis set out in Figure 10.1 could form the basis of a decision tree that would enable the consultant diagnostician to 'read' the output from the MASOD and come to a diagnosis of what needs to be worked on *next* in the organization. This would be analogous to a medical consultant 'reading' the output from a MRI or CT scan to diagnose the source of the illness/ malfunction of a patient to make a decision about the treatment required to 'cure' the condition.

The next step is to validate the whole process. This could be achieved by assembling another database, repeating the categories of variables and adding extra post-treatment ones as appropriate, to ascertain the changes that have taken place. This process is the way ahead for achieving evidence-based diagnosis and treatment.

All this sounds a daunting task. However, help is on its way with all the work currently taking place in the rapidly expanding field of 'big data analytics'. At the moment this appears just to use correlational methods and algorithms to 'mine' large volumes of unstructured information collected about and from working organizations. It would be a relatively easy step in the development of these methods to use the more advanced statistical methods, set out in Figure 10.2, linked by algorithms so that the structured data assembled, as suggested by this book, could be analysed through built-in decision rules to produce findings that would enable diagnostic and validation decisions to be made.

A further useful outcome from having a database that is regularly up-dated is being able to monitor the development of an organization and the effects and effectiveness of the treatments. This reflects the trend in monitoring people as the way ahead for diagnosing early any malfunction of the body, so increasing health and life expectancy. The aim of this book is to achieve this for organizations.

Towards Training and a Professional Qualification

In our view what is needed is for an independent group of consultants to emerge that specialize in organizational diagnoses and who do not have any exclusive connections to treatment suppliers. Perhaps they should have a separate regulatory trade association that might be comparable to the insurance assessors or loss adjusters, honest brokers between organizations and consultants. Similarities would also exist with the earlier rôle of clinical psychologists, before they became involved in therapies they were the experts in diagnosis of mental ills and then passed the patient on to the psychiatrist who did the treatment. Things have changed now, but at least there is still the control over those psychiatrists with a particular leaning towards treating all their patients as if they were suffering from a childhood sexual disorder, or whatever!

These 'Professional Organizational Diagnosticians' would have sufficient expertise and experience with multivariate analysis to be able to interpret the results from orgscans. They will have 'technicians' to carry out the data collection that would feed the computer programs. They would most probably be trained and qualified occupational psychologists with considerable experience in the field of organizational behaviour.

Concluding Comments

It is hoped that the tentative suggestions towards evidence-based decision making made here will encourage further work along this route. Difficult as this may be, surely this conceptual/statistical approach to improving organizational health and fitness through diagnosis and treatment must be the ultimate way ahead? In the meantime it must not be forgotten that the human brain is far more powerful than any computer yet developed for taking in and analysing data, if it is well-trained and well-equipped with nerve cells and fast, non-corrupting synapses and if used in a systematic and disciplined way, thinking managers and organizational diagnosticians have a good chance of getting right the decision about what an organization should be doing differently next and what treatment it should use to bring about the change. Although these decisions can still be regarded as 'subjective' this 'disciplined subjectivity' is an intermediate step beyond 'enlightened subjectivity' in making diagnoses.

Thus while the development of an evidence-based approach should further improve the quality of diagnosis, the preceding chapters have described other approaches to improving organizational fitness that are already available to those who want to make things better in an organization.

Appendix A

Signs and Signals of Organizational Illness and Health

In spite of the lack of an agreed approach or classification of organizational problems involving people, much has been written about the kinds of information that can be used to decide whether or not a work organization is functioning well. Some possible 'key indicators' have been developed from many points of view. In financial terms, such things as earnings per share, turnover, profit, return on capital employed and unit cost are used. In social terms, length of existence, growth, esteem and influence are used as indices of effectiveness. In behavioural terms, the presence or absence of industrial action such as strikes, productivity, job satisfaction, absenteeism, labour turnover and the education, knowledge and skill of the workforce can all be viewed as 'vital signs'.

In an organizational setting, some behavioural 'key indicators' may already exist but in our view they do need to be interpreted with care. For example, in motor manufacturing there are statistics about the numbers of people involved in the manufacturing of vehicles so that the efficiency of plants can be compared on the basis of numbers of people employed compared with the numbers of cars produced. However, there is also an increasing trend for complete sub-units to be built by suppliers before delivery to the production plant. So while the number of employees needed in a final assembly plant that is being supplied with assembled sub-units may appear to be lower, more information is required before the plant's true efficiency can be calculated.

Records of attendance and absenteeism may also exist but again require careful investigation. For example, some studies of coalminers' attendance records showed that absenteeism tended to increase with the number of hours worked – in other words absenteeism was directly related to the amount of overtime that had been worked.

Personnel records may also yield potentially important information about the age, education, knowledge and skill levels of the workforce. But often such records are based on application forms completed at the time of employment and have not been kept up to date – those who have applied for an 'Investor's in People Award' will know that that it can be important to remind employees of the on-the-job and other training that they have received before the formal assessment process takes place. Questions also need to be asked about whether the skills possessed by the current workforce meet current and foreseeable requirements or whether they are associated with yesterday's technology? Could at least some of the workforce retrain and acquire new skills if alternative work could be found?

Those investigating organizational ill-health also need to consider whether they have sufficient information to be sure that the key problems have been identified and to form, a 'base line' for assessing the impact of any remedial action. There can be many different signs and signals that indicate that organizations, or parts of an organization, are 'sick', 'healthy' or even displaying 'fitness'. Walking around some organizations seeing happy faces, jaunty steps even a 'buzz' can be sensed to indicate all is well and good work is trying to be done. Then, in others, there are sullen faces and apparent lethargy and misery.

Much has been written about the kinds of information that can be used to decide whether or not a work organization is functioning well. Their sicknesses can be due to their 'structure', for example, layers of management, decision-making procedures, control systems, reporting assignments, etc.; or the way that the people in the organization are behaving, for example, management style, interpersonal relationships, lack of concern and recognition, etc. In the main body of this book we have been warning that a common mistake in organizational and individual investigations and treatments is to attempt to treat behavioural problems with structural treatments and structural problems with behavioural treatments. So, for example, while it might be possible to re-organize work so that someone who finds it difficult to attend to detail has less detailed work to do, a better solution might be to help the individual to find ways of coping with the requirements of the current situation.

An even greater difficulty exists when attempting to 'add up' these signs and signals so that some kind of diagnosis can be made that an organization is 'sick' or 'healthy'. A similar difficulty also exists with people. When is a person mentally 'normal' or 'abnormal'? It is easier to start work first at the extremes. Diagnostic manuals to aid this process usually make use of some kind of check-list.

All that said, the kind of list that has been put forward for organizations can be illustrated as follows:

Some Characteristics of 'Healthy/Fit' and 'Unhealthy/Sick' Organizations

HEALTHY/FIT

1. Objectives are widely shared by the members and there is a strong and consistent movement toward those objectives.

2. People feel free to signal their awareness of difficulties because they expect the problems to be dealt with and they are optimistic that they can be solved.

3. Problem-solving is highly pragmatic. In attacking problems, people work informally and are not preoccupied with status, territory or second-guessing 'what higher management will think'.

4. The points of decision making are determined by such factors as ability, sense of responsibility, availability of information, workload, timing and requirements for professional and management development. Organizational level as such is not considered a factor.

5. There is a noticeable sense of team play in planning, in performance and in discipline – in short, a sharing of responsibility.

6. The judgment of people lower down in the organization is respected.

7. The range of problems tackled includes personal needs and relationships.

8. Collaboration is freely entered into. People readily request the help of others and are willing to give in turn. Ways of helping one another are highly developed. Individuals and groups compete with one another, but they do so fairly and in the direction of a shared goal.

9. When there is a crisis, the people quickly band together in work until the crisis departs.

10.   Conflicts are considered important to decision making and personal growth. They are dealt with effectively, in the open. People say what they want and expect others to do the same.

11.   There is a great deal of on-the-job learning based on a willingness to give, seek and use feedback and advice. People see themselves and others as capable of significant personal development and growth.

12.   Joint critique of progress is routine.

13.   Relationships are honest. People do care about one another and do not feel alone.

14.   People are 'turned-on' and highly involved by choice. They are optimistic. The workplace is important and fun (why not?).

15.   Leadership is flexible, shifting in style and approach to suit the situation.

16.   There is a high trust in one another and a sense of freedom and mutual responsibility. People generally know what is important to the organization and what is not.

17.   Risk is accepted as a condition of growth and change.

18.   Learning, rather than punishment, arises from each mistake.

19.   Poor performance is confronted and a joint resolution sought.

20.   Organization structure, procedures and policies are fashioned to help people get the job done and to protect the long-term health of the organization. They are also readily changed.

21.   There is a sense of order, and yet a high rate of innovation. Old methods are questioned and often give way.

22.   The organization itself adapts swiftly to opportunities or other changes in its marketplace because every pair of eyes is watching and every head is anticipating the future.

23.   Frustrations are the call to action. 'It is my/our responsibility to save the ship', is the response to crises.

24.   The views of the 'boss' (or other appointed leader) are frequently but respectfully challenged.

25.   Non-conforming behaviour is tolerated.

UNHEALTHY/SICK

1.   Little personal investment in organizational objectives, except at top levels.

2.   People in the organization see things go wrong and do nothing about it. Nobody volunteers. Mistakes and problems are habitually hidden or shelved.

3.   Status and boxes on the organization chart are more important than solving the problem.

4.   People at the top try to control as many decisions as possible. They become bottlenecks, and make decisions with inadequate information and advice.

5.   Managers feel alone in trying to get things done. Somehow orders, policies and procedures do not get carried out as intended.

6.   The judgment of people lower down in the organization is not respected outside the narrow limits of their jobs.

7.   Personal needs and feelings are side issues.

8.   People compete when they need to collaborate. They are very jealous of their area of responsibility. Seeking or accepting help is felt to be a sign of weakness. Offering help is unthought of. People distrust each other's motives and speak poorly of one another – the manager tolerates this.

9.   When there is a crisis, people withdraw or start blaming each other.

10.   Conflict is mostly covert and managed by office politics and other games, or there are interminable and irreconcilable arguments.

11.   Learning is difficult. People do not approach their peers to learn from them – have to learn from own mistakes – reject experience of others. They get little feedback on performance, and much of that is not helpful.

12.   Feedback is avoided.

13.   Relationships are contaminated by image building. People feel alone and lack concern for one another. There is an undercurrent of fear.

14.   People feel locked into their jobs. They feel stale and bored but constrained by the need for security. Their behaviour, for example in staff meetings, is listless and docile. It is not much fun. They get their kicks elsewhere.

15.   The manager is a prescribing father to the organization.

16.   The manager tightly controls small expenditures and demands excessive justification. He allows little freedom for making mistakes.

17.   Minimizing risk is a very high value.

18.   One mistake and you are out!

19.   Poor performance is glossed over or handled arbitrarily.

20.   People take refuge in policies and procedures, and play games with organization structure.

21.   Tradition is more important than change.

22.   Innovation is not widespread – in the hands of a few.

23.   Appraisal interviews are disliked.

24.   People swallow their frustrations. 'I can do nothing. It is their responsibility to save the ship. Let them get on with it!'.

25.   People talk about 'work' or 'office' troubles at home or in the corridors and car parks, not with those involved.

26.   People treat each other in a formal and polite manner that masks issues – especially with the boss. Nonconformity is frowned upon.

The above can be regarded as a starting point for building up a check-list of symptoms which will help the broad diagnoses of organizational health.

Appendix B

When Individuals Threaten the Future of the Organization

A special case of organization malfunction or sickness is when the root cause can be traced to a single individual at any level in an organization. This appendix will explore this possibility.

For the main part of the book we have assumed that the behaviour of managers and those they manage is both reasonable and rational. However there are clearly times when that is not the case.

Those investigating problems and trying to manage them must keep at the back of their mind the possibility that owners and other managers may be spiteful or vindictive and that some shop-floor and other employees may not wish to conform. At worst, features of work and working conditions which have been acceptable to the majority of employees may suddenly become the focus of complaints whipped up by a zealous union representative whose ultimate agenda is the overthrow of capitalist society. Equally, morale may be destroyed as staff are alienated by a short-tempered manager or one that makes lewd and other inappropriate suggestions to staff. Hopefully these issues would have surfaced when working through, probably within a formal appraisal interview, the outcomes of the 'Diagnostic Model for People Management' set out in Figure 5.3 in Chapter 5. If this process does not resolve the issues a more drastic approach will need to be taken.

The following comments come from a former senior manager in a major company which at one stage appeared to have far more than its fair share of industrial relations problems. Invited to give some insight into how managers tried to deal with such situations, he has done so on the understanding that he remains anonymous.

Rogues and Villains

There are sometimes employees, usually in larger companies, that can cause employers trouble. Even though employment legislation has tended to curb excessively disruptive behaviour there can still be problems.

Any experienced HR manager will come across the rogue. His conduct, rogues are usually male, may verge on the insolent, over the top altercations with the supervisor, poor attendance and timekeeping, and behaviour frequently meriting dismissal.

The solution may not be found by carefully following the approved disciplinary code for one of several reasons. The employee may be popular and/ or a particular friend of a shop steward. Sometimes there is sympathy as there is rumour that the loss of his job would severely affect his family where one of his children is seriously ill. When matters normally dictate an oral warning should be given followed by further stages in the disciplinary procedure, the situation can be fraught with difficulties. There might be more complications if managers believe it is not the time to risk industrial action. As HR managers know, there are rarely times when it is convenient.

Whatever action is taken, it will be necessary for management to steel itself for possible disruption, even if only for a short period. The behaviour of a rogue employee is unlikely to change. Matters might improve naturally but if not, supervision and HR officers must be alerted to ensure subsequent recordable misdemeanours are logged and proper tribunal-proof action is taken if they occur. With luck and careful management, repercussions will be minimized.

Villains prove a greater threat. In many societies as well as trade unions, persuading the sensible to stand for office can be difficult. This can result at national and local level in the election of those who have their own or fringe political party agenda. These agenda can have nothing in common with the well-being of the company or even employees. They can consist of pay demands exceeding the total net profits for the next 10 years, the overthrow of the political system or even the arming of the workers marching on the courts.

Symptoms of the problem are obvious, the most common being sporadic walkouts and threats of walkouts on the most trifling of pretexts. Occasionally fate can happily intervene. The villains have to be active and may even be caught by the police damaging the roof of the car at someone else's picket line! Hopefully, the workforce, or their spouses, will tire of losing pay and will rebel. If not, in the longer term it might be possible to persuade a more suitable employee to stand for election. In the short term a more drastic measure and management needs to be brave is, after a walkout, to send employees home for an additional shift. This can have a salutary effect on shop-floor thinking, a shock to the system, a realization that strong arm tactics are not the sole prerogative of the workforce. Confidence in the villain may be lessened and may hasten his demise.

None of the suggestions above are foolproof. Careful selection is important in the first place. If a villain or rogue has crept under the wire, a careful examination of his application for employment for all omissions and accuracy may be useful. Solutions can only be found by imaginative and occasionally unorthodox treatment.

Notes on Chapters

Chapter 1

A prequel for this book can be read at: Randell, Gerry (1998). Organisational sicknesses and their treatment. *Management Decision, 36, 1*.

Chapter 2

It is difficult to be precise about when the first systematic efforts were made to identify and treat organizational problems. A thorough and fascinating history of management is set out in: Urwick, L. (ed.) (1956). *The Golden Book of Management: A Historical Record of the Life and Work of Seventy Pioneers*. London: Newman Neame. The book, sponsored by the International Committee of Scientific Management, starts with:

> The history of modern management is often considered to begin with F.W. Taylor in the United States at the turn of the present century (i.e. 1899).
>
> Records preserved by good fortune, however, show interesting anticipation of scientific management in one or two countries by a century or more. In Great Britain, in particular, it could be claimed that the first illustration of scientific management in action is to be found from 1795 onwards, in the Soho Engineering Foundry near Birmingham of Boulton, Watt & Company (of steam engine fame) .... In the Soho Foundry at that time the following management techniques were being consciously applied, on a small scale but nevertheless no less systematically than in modern concerns today.

The list included, 'A workers' training scheme', 'Work study', 'Payment by results based on work study', 'Provision for personnel welfare, with a sickness benefit scheme administered by an elected committee of employees', and 'An executive development scheme'.

The next pioneer described in the book is social reformer and philanthropist, Robert Owen. In an essay, third of many, addressed to 'the superintendents of manufactories' in 1813, he wrote:

> *Many of you have long experienced in your manufacturing operations the advantages of substantial, well-contrived and well-executed machinery ... If, then, due care as to the state of your inanimate machines can produce such beneficial results, what may not be expected if you devote equal attention to your vital machines, which are far more wonderfully constructed? When you shall acquire a right knowledge of these, of their curious mechanism, of their self-adjusting powers; when the proper main-spring shall be applied to their varied movements – you will become conscious of their real value, and you will readily be induced to turn your thoughts more frequently from your inanimate to your living machines; you will discover that the latter may be easily trained and directed to procure a large increase in pecuniary gain, while you may also derive from them high and substantial gratification.*

Owen applied the above principles to the textile mill, making mainly sail cloth, that he had taken over from his father-in-law at New Lanark in Scotland. He became very successful financially and famous as a social reformer. He is considered to be the father of personnel management. The New Lanark mills are now a UNESCO World Heritage site (as is Titus Salt's model village Saltaire). He can be read at: Claeys, G. (ed.) (1991). *Robert Owen: A New View of Society and other Writings*. London: Penguin Books.

There is a section on all the pioneers of management who developed the early solutions to organizational ills in the *Golden Book of Management*.

The first classification of treatments appeared in German in 1912, and was then published in English as: Münsterberg, H. (1913). *Psychology and Industrial Efficiency*. Boston, MA: Houghton Mifflin.

For descriptions of the more recent 'cures' that are categorized in Chapter 2, most standard text books on personnel management will give an account of them. Particularly thorough is: Sisson, K. (ed.) (1994). *Personnel Management: A Comprehensive Guide to Theory and Practice in Britain*. 2nd edition. Oxford: Blackwell.

A more academic approach to describing treatments can be found in: Arnold, J. and Randall, R., et al. (2010). *Work Psychology: Understanding Human Behaviour in the Workplace*. 5th edition. Harlow: Pearson.

The definitive account of the Hawthorne investigations is: Roethlisberger, F.J. and Dickson, W.J. (1939). *Management and the Worker*. Cambridge, MA: Harvard University Press.

Chapter 3

A useful, straightforward introduction of systems theory applied to management is in: Singleton, W.T. (1981). Systems theory and skill theory, in *Management Skills*, edited by W.T. Singleton. Lancaster: MTP Press.

Figure 3.2 was first set out in a paper to the Occupational Psychology Section of the British Psychological Society in February 1965, it was published as: Randell, G.A. (1966). A systems approach to industrial behaviour. *Occupational Psychology*, 40. It was reprinted in: (1971), *Studies in Organizational Behavior and Management*, edited by D.E. Porter, P.B. Applewhite and M.J. Misshauk. Scranton, NJ: International Textbook Co.

At this time other systems approaches were being made, including: Toplis, J.W. (1970). Studying people at work: Outline of a system. *Occupational Psychology*, 44. This paper detailed situational factors and individual characteristics that can affect behaviour at work, and also detailed possible measures of behaviour and potential sources of information.

The use of Figure 3.1 in management development is described in: Randell. G.A. (1981). Management education and training, in *Management Skills*, edited by W.T. Singleton. Lancaster: MTP Press.

A more recent publication which is closest to the concepts outlined in this book is: Brach, A.P. (2002). *How Organizations Work: Taking a Holistic Approach to Enterprise Health*. New York: Wiley.

Chapter 4

This, and later chapters, are much influenced by the work of Charles Kepner and Ben Tregoe in the 1960s. Their best-selling book of 1965, *The Rational*

Manager was updated as: Kepner, C.H. and Tregoe, B.B. (1997). *The New Rational Manager*. Princeton, NJ: Princeton University Press.

The original *Rational Manager* focussed on Problem Analysis, whereas *The New Rational Manager* also addressed Decision Analysis and Potential Problem Analysis.

Another influential book that has recently been updated is: Senge, P. (2006). *The Fifth Discipline*. London: Random House.

Empirical research which advocates using 'behaviourally anchored rating scales' (BARS) to measure performance at work more objectively is described in: Bailey, C.T. (1983). *The Measurement of Job Performance*. Aldershot: Gower.

A wide-ranging book which focuses on employee involvement in organizations is: Siedman, D. (2011). *HOW: Why How we do Anything Means Everything*. Expanded edition. New York: Wiley.

A less philosophical and more statistically supported account of Seidman's work can be found in: 'The HOW Report: New metrics for a new reality', available at: http://www.lrn.com/howmetrics/data/LRNHowReport2012.pdf

The lead in employee engagement in the UK is taken by the 'Great Place to Work Institute' (www.greatplacetowork.co.uk) who publish an annual survey of those companies in the UK who display most employee engagement.

A controversial and insightful book on engagement is: Smythe, J. (2007). *The CEO: Turning Hierachy Upside Down to Drive Performance*. Aldershot: Gower.

A very recent book that examines the decision to speak out in organizations, or to keep quiet, is: Burke, R.J. and Cooper, C.L. (eds) (2013). *Voice and Whistleblowing in Organizations: Overcoming Fear, Fostering Courage and Unleashing Candour*. Northampton, MA: Edward Elgar Publishing.

Chapter 5

Checklists are widely used by airline pilots and engineers and are being taken up in the human resources industry, see: Critical Appraisal Skills Programme (www.casp-uk.net), see also The Team Diagnostic Check List (www.mindtools. com).

A very useful description of the diagnostic schemes mentioned in Chapter 5 is given in: Fallatta, S. (2008). *Organizational Diagnostic Models: A Review and a Synthesis*. Available at http://www.leadersphere.co./img/orgmodels.pdf

There are many guides available on-line to carrying out a Root Cause Analysis (RCA). A compact and clear guide is available from BRC Global Standards, London, at: www.brcglobalstandards.com/LinkClick.aspx?file ticket=BkP7K

An easy to follow book on Root Cause Analysis is: Ammerham, M. (1997). *Root Cause Analysis: A Simplified Approach to Identifying and Reporting Workplace Errors*. New York: Productivity Press.

The 'classic' book on organizational diagnosis is: Weisbord, M.R. (1978). *Organizational Diagnosis: A Workbook of Theory and Practice*. New York: Perseus Books.

The use of Figure 5.3 in management skills training was described in: Randell. G.A. (1981). Management education and training, in *Management Skills*, edited by W.T. Singleton. Lancaster: MTP Press.

Chapter 6

The Kepner and Tregoe and the Peter Senge books (see Chapter 4) also underpin much of the material in this chapter.

A review of the issues underpinning effective appraisal schemes can be found in Randell, G. (1984). Employee appraisal, in *Personnel Management: A Comprehensive Guide to Theory and Practice in Britain*. 2nd edition. Keith Sisson. Oxford: Blackwell.

Chapter 7

The debate on the merits and downsides of 'Top-down' versus 'Bottom-up' management goes back a long way, and is still active, especially in CIPD circles, today. It was probably begun by: Lupton, T. (1971). Organizational change: Top-down or bottom-up management. *Personnel Review*, 1, 1.

Two contrasting analyses of Bottom-up/Top-down management can be seen in: Strebel, P. (ed.) (2000). *Focused Energy: Mastering Bottom-up Organization*. Chichester: Wiley. See also, Quirke, B. (2008). *Making the Connection: Using Internal Communications to Turn Strategy into Action*. Revised edition. Aldershot: Gower.

An influential book with chapters by many of the current gurus of management has a chapter of much relevance to this book: Beer, M. (2003). Building organizational fitness, in *Organization 21 C: Some Day all Organizations will Lead this Way*, edited by S. Chowdhury. London: Financial Times Prentice Hall.

This chapter inspired a submission, 'Organizational Fitness and Renewal', to the Australian Public Service Commission to help them become 'the best public service anywhere in the world'. It can be usefully read at: www.dpmc.gov.au/consultation/aga_reform/pdfs/0108%20RTW.pdf

A powerful article that builds on Michael Beer's work at Harvard and provides a 'systemic scorecard' for measuring and evaluating organizational fitness programmes is: Voelpel, S.C., Liebold, M. and Mahmoud, K.M. (2003). The organizational fitness navigator: Enabling and measuring organizational fitness for rapid change. *Journal of Change Management*, 4(2), 123–40.

Chapter 8

This chapter is based on the work of the Human Resources Research Group, based at The Bradford Management Centre from 1970–97, which has been named 'The Bradford Approach to Leadership'. The central concept behind this work is that interacting purposefully and effectively with people and organizations requires considerable interpersonal skill.

The key publications are:

Randell, G. (2008). The core of leadership. *Business Leadership Review*, V:III.

Wright, P.L. (1996). *Managerial Leadership*. London: Routledge.

Taylor, D.S. and Wright, P.L. (1988). *Developing Interpersonal Skills: Through Tutored Practice.* Hemel Hempstead: Prentice Hall.

Wright, P.L. and Taylor, D.S. (1984). *Improving Leadership Performance.* Hemel Hempstead: Prentice Hall.

Randell, G.A. (1981). Management education and training, in *Management Skills,* edited by W.T. Singleton. Lancaster: MTP Press.

Various unpublished Ph.D. theses available at the University of Bradford Library also underpin the material of this chapter, notably:

Alban Metcalf, B. (1982). *Micro-skills of Leadership: A multivariate analysis of the perceptions of 78 managers and 78 subordinates immediately following a standard rôle-played, recorded appraisal interview, to discover those verbal behaviours which determine more effective behaviour.*

Johnston, T. (1990). *Leadership skills in work teams: An empirical study of the micro-skills of leadership in working teams focusing on problem solving, participation, supportiveness and goal setting as the key components of effective group performance.*

Callaghan, C. (1991). *Verbal leader behaviour in manager-subordinate interactions: An investigation of conversational processes in rôle-played dyadic interactions using static and sequential analysis techniques.*

Baverstock, S. (1994). *Managing the emotions of others in the workplace:* An investigation of communication behaviours associated with emotion handling in simulated manager-subordinate interactions.

The online resource www.mindtools.com provide, mainly for free, a very comprehensive account of leadership theories and skills. However they make it all sound too easy.

The terms 'personal mastery' and 'learning organization' were used by Peter Senge (Chapter 4)

A very powerful, all encompassing, and British too, text book on leadership is: Gill, R. (2011). *Theory and Practice of Leadership.* 2nd edition. London: Sage.

Chapter 9

There appear to be large and potentially important differences in views about what is involved in 'Internal Communications'. Some see it as an area of expertise requiring skills associated with public relations and journalism, as in the following book: Quirke, B. (2008). *Making the Connections: Using Internal Communications to Turn Strategy into Action*. Revised edition. Aldershot: Gower.

As a result of carrying out attitude surveys and other studies of people at work, Psychologists take a much wider view. In such surveys, employees comment on communications from a wide range of sources including managers and colleagues, those in other departments, suppliers and customers. In a study analysing a large number of such surveys, the common theme emerged that people want to know where they stand, particularly in times of crisis, see: Buzzard, R.B. (1966). Security or knowing where you stand. *NIIP Bulletin*, August 3–12

A balanced analysis of the processes and procedures making up 'employee voice' is in the last section of the Keith Sisson edited book referred to under Chapter 2 in this section.

The theories that underpin human communication can get very heavy. A useful introduction is: Griffin, E. (2011). *A First Look at Communication Theory*. New York: McGraw Hill.

The HRRG at Bradford also carried out research on the 'micro-skills' of communication. The research was focussed on how to write memoranda and emails that would result in the staff of an organization 'feeling communicated'.

The relevant Ph.D. thesis in the University of Bradford Library is: Broadfield, A. (1997). *The Micro-processes of Change: Written communication skills for organiational change; An analysis of how written memoranda should be constructed and circulated to increase the chances of acceptance and commitment to organisational change within manufacturing and service companies.*

Another thesis explored the importance of managers showing concern for their staff to the quality of communication between them; Morgan, P. (1995). *Managerial concern in context, the demonstration of concern, individual differences and organisational culture; an investigation, by questionnaire, into the degree to which contextual factors, organisational culture and two personality traits have upon the demonstration of concern by managers in a variety of organisational settings.*

A further thesis concentrated on how opposition to change can affect the quality of diagnostic decision-making in working groups, by: Lynch, S. (2002). *Decision making in working groups*: A multivariate analysis of psychometric data of individuals, group membership and interactive processes of managers in decision-making simulations, focussing on the impact of oppositional behaviour on the quality of decisions.

Again, the resource www.mindtools.com put forward a useful checklist where they say communication, through all types of media, should be:

Clear. Concise. Concrete. Correct. Coherent. Complete. Courteous.

Chapter 10

The origins of this book can be found in research carried out at Birkbeck College, University of London in the 1960s, written up in: Randell, G.A. (1972). *An Application of Scientific and Technological Concepts to a Problem of Worker Behaviour*. Unpublished Ph.D. thesis, University of London Library.

Some of the findings from this research were published in: Randell, G.A. (1975). The use of tests and scored questionnaires in salesmen selection, in *Psychological Testing in Personnel Assessment*, edited by Kenneth M. Miller. Epping: Gower Press.

The methodology used in this research was much influenced by: Cattell, R.B. (ed.) (1966). *Handbook of Multivariate Experimental Psychology*. Chicago, IL: Rand McNally.

A highly regarded starter for SPSS is: Field, A. (2000). *Discovering Statistics Using SPSS for Windows*. London: Sage.

There are many books on the use of multivariate analysis in decision making, most are very demanding. One that is closest to the approach set out in Chapter 10 is: Mertler, C.A. and Vannatta, R.A. (2002). *Advanced and Multivariate Statistical Methods*. 2nd edition. Los Angeles, CA: Pyrczak Publishing.

One of the many books recently published on big data is: Minelli, M., Chambers, M. and Dhiraj, A. (2013). *Big Data, Big Analytics: Emerging Business Intelligence and Analytic Trends for Today's Businesses*. Hoboken, NJ: Wiley.

Index

360° feedback 20, 80

academic publications 123
additional information
    need for 44–5
analysis paralysis 44, 85
appraisal interview 64, 69–70, 101–2,
    110, 138, 141, 151
apprentices 31
Assessment Centre Procedure 82
assessment of the attributes of
    employees 36–7
authoritarianism
    leadership, and 104–5

Bedlam hospital 15
behavioural treatments 17, 19–22, 134
bonuses 19, 102
Boulton, Matthew 13
business process re-engineering 18

'care in the community' 3, 13
    See Salt, Titus
classification of treatments 16–17, 146
coaching 20–21
communications of 31–2
    importance of 31–2
confidentiality 47, 79
    assurances of 42–3, 54–5, 70–71
constants 30
consultants 4, 14, 17–18, 23, 57, 91–2,
    105, 109, 115, 131
    external consultants 27, 48
    medical consultants 24

organizational fitness, and 91–2
co-ownership 18
cope in the community 15–16
counselling 17, 20–21

database 126–7, 130
    development of 126–7
developing environment, equipment
    and methods 87
diagnosis 2, 6–7, 51–66
    activities 53
    approaches 52–3
    closed system of main interactions
        and problems 60
    collecting information, expertise
        and 57
    conclusions 7
    content of work 61
    context of work 61
    current approaches fit for purpose,
        whether 58–9
    difficulty of carrying out 58–9
    emerging views 43–4
    evidence-based 10
    form of work 61
    framework for 62
    historical information 58
    history 52–3
    level of work organization 62
    linking symptoms and causes 57–8
    local, not attempted or incorrect
        56–7
    meaning 53
    medical doctors, and 2

model for people management
    63–4
motivation, and 64–5
multi-stage iterative process 50
previous problems, and 40
problems traced to specific
    locations or groups 57
questions to inform 39–45
remedial action required 69–72
resistance to investigation 59
scenarios to illustrate 54–6
size of problem 60
structure of organization 61
symptoms, and 53
systems approaches 7, 60–65
techniques 52
using models in practice 65
whole process 38–9
displaying good intentions towards
    the staff 21–2
DSM-1 124
DSM-IV 124–5

EFQM Excellence Model 80
'employee voice' 111–12, 152
'Employer Brand' 30
engagement 22, 45, 72, 78, 80–81, 92,
    95, 104, 112, 126, 148
    employee engagement 8, 21, 148
    encouraging engagement 42–3
    'Transactional Engagement' 78
    'Transformational Engagement' 78
evaluation 8, 44, 46–47, 56, 68, 75, 85,
    88, 93, 116–17
evidence-based decision making 131–2
external factors 5, 29

failing appraisal scheme 69–70
falling sales 73
fashionable solutions 3–4, 13–22, 67,
    75, 123

history 13–16
"quick fix" 16
'Fault Tree Analysis' 52
'Fishbone Diagram' 52
framework for organizational
    diagnosis 7, 41, 62, 86, 90

General Electric 15
Gilbreth, Frank Bunker 3, 13–14

'Hard' science training 19–20
Harvey-Jones, John 15
Hawthorne investigations 22, 147
Hawthorne studies 68
high labour turnover 38, 40, 54–6, 67
    engineering company 56
    pharmaceutical manufacturing
        staff 54–5
    plastics factory 55–6
Honda 117
how people feel about their work 5,
    35–7
human resources professional
    organizational fitness, and 90–91

IBM SPSS 125–6, 130
inculcating skills in the job 20–21
individuals threatening future of
    organization 141–3
internal communications 9–10, 81,
    111–21
    bottom-up 117–18
    case for co-ordinating change
        119–21
    committees, and 120
    employee voice 111–12
    Honda 117
    initiative overload, and 119–20
    top-down 112–14
    traditional focus 111
    work groups, between 118–19

investigation 45–50
   analysis of information 46
   collating of information 46
   collecting information 45–6
   diagnosis, and 46
   formal meetings 49
   funding 49–50
   independent individuals 48
   information collection phase 47–8
   numbers involved 45–6
   preliminary, usefulness 47
   planning 45
   reporting of information 46
   special team 48
   staffing 47–9
   team 48
   treatment, and 46
Investors in People 13, 19, 80

job and career information
   provision of 86
job design 18
job enrichment 18
job rotation 18

key indicators 27, 133–4

large organizations 23, 25, 30, 32,
      48–9, 112–13, 115, 119
last resort treatment 15
leader
   manager as 29
leadership 8–9, 97–110
   acquiring and developing 107–8
   appraisal interviews, and 101–2
   authoritarianism, and 104–5
   cognitive 9, 100
   common core 98
   components 97
   conflicting needs of stakeholders
      105

criteria for observing and
      measuring 109
   definition 9
   equilibrium, and 106–7
   formal training, and 108
   kinds of 98
   macro skills 105–6
   market forces, and 100
   meaning 97
   motor 9, 100
   nature of 8–9
   non-verbal behaviours and skills
      107
   outcome, as 108–9
   perceptual 100
   rainbow concepts 98–9
   skills 99, 100–103
   types of questions 104
   verbal behaviour 103–7
   vision 106
line manager 20, 41, 80, 89, 93, 113,
      115–16
   organizational fitness, and 89–90
long-term statistical evidence-based
      diagnosis 125–31

management
   questions to inform 39–45
management by objectives 18
management of symptoms 51–2
manager
   leader, as 29
managerial styles and grids 20
Manual for Organizational Diagnosis
      10, 124–5
manufacturing engine of people at
      work 29
MASOD 129–30
Mayo, Elton 21
measures of behaviour at work 35,
      35–6, 77

measures of performance at work 36,
    78
mega approaches 17–18
mental hospitals 15–16
merit rating 19
micro approaches 21–2
midi approaches 19–20
mini approaches 20–21
motivation
    diagnosis, and 64–5
multivariate analysis 10, 125, 127–31,
    153
    interpreting results 128
Multiple problems 72–3

National Health Service 15, 17, 48, 92,
    112, 126
    data-base 126
    see Robinson, Gerry
nationalization 4, 16, 18
neuroleadership 14
neuroses 16–17
Nottingham University 126
    School of Computer Science 126

occupational training, provision of 87
Ofsted 81, 86
open systems 5, 23, 25, 27–32, 62
organization malfunction 25–7, 141
organizational anorexia 30
organizational diagnosis and treatment
    need for 1–11
organizational fitness 8–10, 77–96
    areas that might be improved 86–8
    bottom-up approach 85–6
    consultants, and 91–2
    EFQM Excellence Model 80
    encouraging local dialogue 79
    evaluation 85
    examination of information 84–5
    financial and technical standards 81

follow-up 85
funding of initiatives 95
human resources professional,
    and 90–91
initial objective 84
internal entrepreneurs 78
leadership 8–9
line manager, and 89–90
long-term management of
    programme 94–5
managing bottom-up approach 88
meaning 77
objectives 78
Ofsted 81
Organization-Wide Survey 81
pilot study 84
planning and taking action 85
resilience 78
restructuring, and 82–3
staffing of initiatives 92–4
    audits 92–3
    bottom-up approach 94
    encouraging local dialogue 92
    organizational change 93
    surveys 92–3
    top-down approach 93
taking initiative 83
top-down approach 8, 93
Transactional Engagement 78
using organization change to
    stimulate 82
using surveys and audits to obtain
    additional information 79–82
where to start 88–9
organizational starvation 30
organizational theory 24
organizations
    accumulation of baggage 1
    behavioural sickness 1
    culture 5
    describing 4–5, 23–33

diversity 4–5, 24–5
  impact of 1
  Level A 27
  Level B 26–7
  Level C 26
  understanding 4–5, 23–33
Owen, Robert 3, 13–14, 21, 146
  See 'silent monitors'

patients
  views of 38–9
payment by results 13, 19, 145
performance appraisal 20
performance management 20
personnel selection procedures 86–7
Polizzi, Alex 15
Portas, Mary 15
preparing to diagnose and manage
  problems 5–6, 35–50
presenting problem 39, 43
privatization 4, 16, 18
problem indicators 35–7
processes involving people 28–9
Professional Organizational
  Diagnosticians 10–11, 131
psychological and social working
  conditions, arranging 87–8
psychometrics 41
psychoses 16–17

Quaker chocolate companies 21
quick fixes 40, 50, 89, 109, 123

Ramsey, Gordon 15
rapport
  encouraging 42–3
rating exercise 20
recruitment 30–32, 47, 67
reinforcement 21
  Skinnerian technology 21
restructuring 82–3, 105

rewards 17, 32, 61, 67
  allocating 88
Robinson, Gerry 15
rogues 142
  see villains

Salt, Titus 3, 13–14, 21, 146
  See 'care in the community'
'scientific management' 3, 13–14, 145
  See Taylor, Frederick Winslow
shortage of applications for
  supervisory posts 70–72
signs and signals of organizational
  illness and health 133–9
  attendance records 133
  base line 134
  healthy/fit characteristics 135–7
  key indicators 133–4
  personnel records 134
  structure, and 134
  unhealthy/sick characteristics 137–9
'silent monitors' 3, 13–14
  See Owen, Robert
skills
  acquiring and developing 107–8
  leadership, and 99, 100–103
small organizations 32
sources of information 40–41
supervisory and leadership skills
  20–21
symptoms, verification of 39
systemic diagnosis problems 5–6, 37–8
systems of management 18–19
Systems Thinking
  application 72–3

target setting 18
Taylor, Frederick Winslow 3, 13–14
  See 'scientific management'
telling people where they stand 42,
  152

'Top-down' Deployment 9, 112–14, 118
    capacity and capability of staff
        114–15
    evaluation 117
    launch 116
    monitoring progress 116
    piloting initiatives 115–16
    problems with 112–14
    strategic options 115
    successful, planning 114–17
    training, and 116
Total Quality Management 13, 19, 87
Toyoda, Sakichi 52
Toyota
    5 Whys technique 52
Training Within Industry 13, 20–21
Training and professional
        qualification 131
'Transactional Engagement' 78
'Transformational Engagement' 78
treatment 7–8, 67–76
    considering and taking action 74–5
    direct response 68
    directly related to problems
        identified 68–9
    emerging views 43–4

evaluating 67–76
evaluation 75
failing appraisal scheme 69–70
fashionable 74–5
identifying 67–76
multiple problems 72–3
no cost-effective treatments found
    73–4
practical issues 74
range of issues to be considered 74
scope for improving 67
shortage of applicants for
        supervisory posts 70–72

villains 142–3
virtual organizations 32, 115
Vocational Guidance 31, 86

Watt Jr., James 13
way ahead, the 123–32
Welch, Jack 15
Work Foundation 20
work study 18, 31
worker control 18
worker participation 18
world of work and management 5,
    25–7

If you have found this book useful you may be interested in other titles from Gower

Deception in Selection
Interviewees and the Psychology of Deceit
Max A. Eggert
Hardback: 978-1-4094-4561-6
e-book PDF: 978-1-4094-4562-3
e-book ePUB: 978-1-4094-7477-7

Delivering High Performance
The Third Generation Organisation
Douglas G. Long
Hardback: 978-1-4724-1332-1
e-book PDF: 978-1-4724-1333-8
e-book ePUB: 978-1-4724-1334-5

Human Frailties
Wrong Choices on the Drive to Success
Edited by Ronald J. Burke, Suzy Fox and Cary L. Cooper
Hardback: 978-1-4094-4585-2
e-book PDF: 978-1-4094-4586-9
e-book ePUB: 978-1-4724-0242-4

Measuring Performance
A Toolkit of Traditional and Alternative Methods
David Jenkins
Hardback: 978-0-566-08860-5
e-book PDF: 978-1-4094-4025-3
e-book ePUB: 978-1-4094-5935-4

GOWER

New Demographics New Workspace
Office Design for the Changing Workforce
Jeremy Myerson, Jo-Anne Bichard and Alma Erlich
Hardback: 978-0-566-08854-4
e-book PDF: 978-0-7546-9212-6
e-book ePUB: 978-1-4094-5878-4

Re-Tayloring Management
Scientific Management a Century On
Edited by Christina Evans and Leonard Holmes
Hardback: 978-1-4094-5075-7
e-book PDF: 978-1-4094-5076-4
e-book ePUB: 978-1-4724-0165-6

Risk Strategies
Dialling Up Optimum Firm Risk
Les Coleman
Hardback: 978-0-566-08938-1
e-book PDF: 978-0-566-08939-8
e-book ePUB: 978-1-4094-5953-8

Third Generation Leadership and the Locus of Control
Knowledge, Change and Neuroscience
Douglas G. Long
Hardback: 978-1-4094-4453-4
e-book PDF: 978-1-4094-4454-1
e-book ePUB: 978-1-4094-8329-8

Visit **www.gowerpublishing.com** and

- search the entire catalogue of Gower books in print
- order titles online at 10% discount
- take advantage of special offers
- sign up for our monthly e-mail update service
- download free sample chapters from all recent titles
- download or order our catalogue